Readers will be clamoring for more of Flash as soon as they digest the last story in this powerful and uplifting memoir.

PUBLISHER'S WEEKLY (starred review)

Charming and funny.

CHICAGO TRIBUNE

Stories that teach spiritual lessons, delight with humor, and make me lean in closer to God's heart are my favorites! And this unlikely treasure of a book does just that. You will fall in love with Flash and the way Rachel Anne processes their story together.

LYSA TERKEURST, *New York Times* bestselling author of *The Best Yes* and president of Proverbs 31 Ministries

When I first heard that Rachel Ridge had written a book about her family's donkey, Flash, I had no idea what to expect. Nothing could have prepared me for such a delightful experience! I loved every page of *Flash*, and Rachel has such a gift for storytelling that you can absolutely picture each scene. This book made me laugh at Flash's antics and cry as I identified with the lessons he has taught her family about the way God loves us and sees us. This book will make you fall in love with our Savior all over again and, more than likely, make you hope you can have your own pet donkey someday.

MELANIE SHANKLE, *New York Times* bestselling author of *Sparkly Green Earrings* and *The Antelope in the Living Room*

This book is a delight; it's an honest, funny, and encouraging reminder of the creative, loving ways that God pursues us, teaches us, and changes us. Granted, I never expected that I'd have so much in common with a donkey, but Flash has taught me more than I could have imagined. You're going to love this book, and when you finish reading it, you're going to want to follow Flash's lead and run with horses.

SOPHIE HUDSON, author of *Home Is Where My People Are* and blogger at BooMama.net

Flash is a marvelous, wonderful, funny, touching, and illuminating book. The author makes the good donkey Flash come alive on the pages. I agree with Rachel that God uses all sorts of things—from dogs to donkeys—to teach us more about himself, and all we have to do is pay attention.

JIM KRAUS, bestselling author of *The Dog That Talked to God*

Charming, poignant, funny, honest—Rachel Anne's journey with Flash the donkey is pure reading pleasure as she shares her family's misadventures with their four-legged friend. She opens her heart to us as well, helping us learn memorable lessons about doing life with more meaning and purpose. Flash is delightfully different. I loved it!

LIZ CURTIS HIGGS, bestselling author of *The Girl's Still Got It*

What a charming, endearing, numinous book—and donkey! From the first chapter, you will immediately fall in love with Rachel Anne Ridge and her beloved Flash. By the last line, your eyes will be opened to seeing the ways God shows up and reveals Himself in the most unexpected—and delightful—ways.

LISA WHELCHEL, actress and author of *The Facts of Life* and *Friendship for Grown-Ups*

I always stand amazed at God's infinite creativity. When Rachel and Tom Ridge faced a financial crisis, I would have suggested a financial advisor or career counselor. God chose to send a homeless donkey. Flash used his considerable donkey charm to teach the family lessons about service, faithfulness, purpose, passion, and second chances. You will laugh (often) at the antics of Flash. You will be touched by the authenticity of Rachel's writing and the depth of the lessons God revealed through an abandoned donkey with big ears and a bigger heart.

DAVE BURCHETT, author of *Stay* and *When Bad Christians Happen to Good People*

A kick-in-the-pants read! *Flash* is memoir plus heartwarming and sometimes stressful animal story, mixed together with spiritual truth, all tempered with humor at just the right spots. Though I live in the suburbs, this made me want to disobey my neighborhood's bylaws and get myself a donkey!

MARY DEMUTH, author of *The Wall around Your Heart*

Rachel Ridge has a beautiful ability to take the common things of life (like words) and craft them in such a way that they flow like prose and poetry. Submerging yourself in *Flash* is to become lost in a beautiful gallery of her finest art. With each turn of the page, the master storyteller shares a glimpse of humor, revelation, and hope. We'd all like to have a friend like Flash, faithful and true. I recommend this book to anyone who has ever needed a true-blue friend, a second chance, or a fresh perspective.

JAN GREENWOOD, pastor of Gateway Women (Gateway Church) and author of *Women at War*

I believe that since Creation, God has used animals to teach us about ourselves and about our Creator—if we'll pay attention. Rachel pays attention, and so will her readers as they delight in a quirky and lovable donkey, Flash.

DANDI DALEY MACKALL, author of *Winnie the Horse Gentler*, *Backyard Horses*, and the Starlight Animal Rescue series

What in the world could a donkey teach me about life? Lots. Why? Because donkeys are simple creatures who live simple lives. Isn't simplicity exactly what so many people are seeking to find amid their busy and hectic existences? In the pages of this book, you will find—in the life of Rachel Anne Ridge and in the life of her surprise pet donkey—that simplicity is beautiful.

CHRYSTAL HURST, coauthor of *Kingdom Woman*

Reader, BEWARE! By the end of this book you will be searching for a donkey for your own personal growth! From now on, every time I see one of these marvelous creatures out in the field, I will think of Flash, and I am sure a smile or giggle will follow, for this burro of burden is laden with humor and wisdom. Rachel has dignified a lowly creature to the point that you think it almost necessary to fence in your yard, buy some hay, and wait for the lessons to begin.

TINA WESSON, *Survivor: The Australian Outback* (Season Two) winner

I loved this whimsical, vulnerable, and simply profound book! Rachel tells how a broken, lost, and stubborn animal awakened her awareness of God's voice in her life. Her story gives hope to anyone who has ever felt inadequate or unseen. She takes the simple and makes it shine to encourage the reader to look with a fresh perspective at the potential God puts in each of us.

PAIGE C. GREENE, director of Adult Events, LifeWay Christian Resources

Bravo to Rachel Ridge for this beautifully written book that so eloquently reminds us that our everyday happenings in life can be great lessons and blessings in disguise from our Maker—even in the form of a donkey! Two things you will want when you turn the last page are a donkey in your yard and Rachel as one of your besties!

CINDY OWEN, Given Entertainment Group

Flash

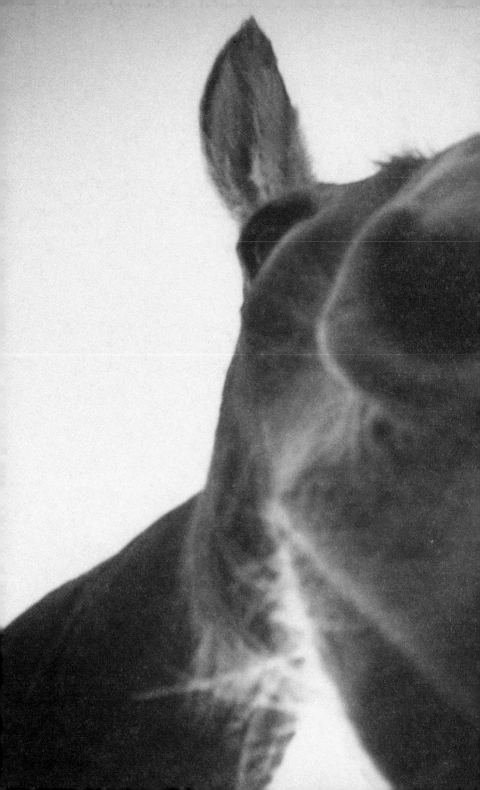

RACHEL ANNE RIDGE

Flash

The Homeless Donkey Who Taught Me
about Life, Faith, and Second Chances

TYNDALE®
MOMENTUM

An Imprint of Tyndale House Publishers, Inc.

Library of Congress Cataloging-in-Publication Data

Ridge, Rachel Anne.
   Flash : the homeless donkey who taught me about life, faith, and second chances / Rachel Anne Ridge.
      pages cm
      ISBN 978-1-4143-9783-2 (hc)
   1. Animals—Religious aspects—Christianity. 2. Human-animal relationships. 3. Donkeys— Miscellanea. I. Flash (Donkey) II. Title.
      BV4596.A54R53 2015
      242—dc23   2015000012

ISBN 978-1-4143-9784-9 (sc)

Printed in the United States of America

21   20   19   18   17   16
6   5   4   3   2   1

For Tom,
my best friend.

And for
Lauren, Meghan, and Grayson,
my greatest gifts.

Contents

Foreword

Good books are like good friends—difficult to find. Many can look promising at the beginning, only to disappoint somewhere down the line. Even when a book is recommended by a person you trust, you can never be sure you'll experience the same connection, that the two of you will hit it off.

Yet sometimes—often for reasons you can't quite put a finger on—you choose to open it up, and open yourself up to it. And every now and then, you're surprised and thankful at the warmth, the joy, the excitement and pleasure you discover inside.

I've had the privilege of finding both—good books *and* good friends. And I'm giddy with joy to introduce you to a couple of them.

Rachel came into my life over a decade ago with a friendship so pure and lasting and impactful that it has made me a better person. Not in theory but in real, tangible, practical ways. She's taught me how to look for and discover the profound beauty tucked away in simplicity, the lovely details that someone else might miss because they're too busy or too tired or too self-absorbed to care.

These little nuances of life are Rachel's treasures. I've watched her take the mundane and routine, the commonplace and plain, and squeeze drops of surprising goodness and vitality from them until everyone in her sphere is saturated with hope and love. She recreates what others would discard, turning it into something memorable and worth capturing. From her perspective, everything is budding with endless and immense possibility.

So a decade ago when she drove up to an unkempt 1970s farmhouse, she saw only the blossoming potential of a cozy, tender place her family could call home. And she loved it and cared for it until it was.

Years later, when her second daughter met the man of her dreams, Rachel transformed a weed-filled, neglected acre of ground into a lush carpet of greenery arched with luxurious foliage to welcome 250 guests and a walk down the aisle.

And the reception. *Oh, the reception!* A timeworn, misshapen barn became a vintage paradise hung with chandeliers and dainty, twinkling white lights that seemed to dance to the beat of the music, like fluffs of white dandelions, blown loose from their stems and carried away on the evening breeze.

This is Rachel's way. Creating goodness where there seems to be none in sight.

And so when Flash showed up—when he sauntered up her quarter-mile driveway, lost, dazed, frightened, and wondering where his next meal would come from—he'd just moseyed unaware into the wide-open arms of grace. Into the arms of Rachel Ridge. The one who sees beauty everywhere and in everything. Even in a dirty, hungry, unwanted, displaced donkey.

He was home.

Rachel and her husband, Tom, looked for Flash's owner for

a while. I mean, can you blame them? Who needs a donkey around to brush and feed and take care of? But then days folded into weeks, and those weeks disappeared into months, and suddenly years had gone by—and Flash was a permanent fixture. Yard art, as she likes to call him. He morphed from a project into a pet, then into a passion, and finally . . . into a present.

A gift. First to her, and then from her to you. And to me.

And the thing is, Flash *is* a gift. I never thought I'd be the kind of girl who could warm up to a donkey, but Flash stole my heart, as well as the hearts of my three sons, who decided he was their own personal pet from the very first day. His penchant for following close behind them with his soft muzzle nudging the backs of their shoulders, begging to be rubbed and caressed, is the highlight of their time with him. Flash keeps his head so close to theirs that they basically bump. They love it. They love him. When my boys show up at the gate and call his name, he comes trotting up enthusiastically. He's been looking for them, waiting for them. And they've been waiting for him.

Turns out we all were and just didn't know it.

Because with Flash, the life lessons weren't long in coming. Rachel would tell me about how he was always able to escape through the one solitary hole in his mile-long fence. Or about the friends he'd made with critters in the next pasture and his sometimes obstinate refusal to move one inch, no matter how hard anyone tugged on his halter. Or his relationship with Beau, the family's beautiful yellow Lab, and how they finally made nice after a long-standing feud.

With each new adventure has come a new lesson, a new gem to enhance all of our lives. Images and insights that could easily go unnoticed by someone less observant and interested. But

Rachel sees all the splendor hidden in these regular simplicities of life. She captures details and digs for beauty, paying attention and causing others to do the same.

Which, by the way, is also the essence of good writing.

And that's exactly what you are holding in your hands. Rachel's good, good writing.

We're so grateful to Tom and Rachel for turning an interruption into an opportunity, for giving a stray donkey a new home and a new name, for letting Flash into their lives. Because in doing so, they let him into ours.

And now, Rachel's letting him into yours.

Every lesson you'll find tucked into these pages will make you laugh, just as much as it will make you learn. And when you turn the final page, you'll be surprised to discover you've found two things in one: a good book about a donkey named Flash, and a good friend in a simple country gal named Rachel.

And you'll never look at either of them quite the same again.

Flash's fan,
Priscilla Shirer

Prologue

The idea had seemed so solid. Or at the very least, romantic. My husband, Tom, and I launched an art and mural business in the Dallas–Fort Worth area during the booming early 2000s. . . . What could possibly go wrong? Gated communities filled with European-styled mansions were springing up everywhere as the good economic times rolled in. An insatiable demand for the best of everything in amenities and decor kept us booked for months at a time creating interior masterpieces for discriminating clients.

Not bad for a company that had started as my little hobby, painting up birdhouses and selling them in local shops. "Dream Big" was my highly original, personal motto. And it had been my dream to make enough money to get my hair highlighted regularly without dipping into the family grocery budget. *Good grief, those highlights are expensive.* That was about as lofty as my early goals had been. I stayed home with three children, desperately needing this creative outlet, while Tom worked long hours in the electronics manufacturing field.

When the phone began to ring with requests for bigger and grander painting projects, suddenly my hobby became more than I could handle. I needed help to pull it off, and my husband was just the person to bring in. Tom loved creating art with me on nights and weekends, lending his talents and muscle power, since by now scaffolds and lifting heavy supplies were involved. As a creative spirit stuck in a precisely controlled industry, he secretly longed for a way to leave the corporate treadmill and do something with his artistic talents. And when Tom's job evaporated in an industry downturn, it appeared to be the perfect time to launch our dream together.

It *had* to be divine providence, right?

So it was, indeed, a good moment to start a venture we had no prior training in. We would wing it.

We wanted to create beautiful things and paint stuff and make people happy. It was a simple dream. And it worked, mostly. Yes, the cyclical nature of the housing market challenged us more than we anticipated. We knew that "feast and famine" seasons were prerequisites for entrepreneurial triumph. But doing what we loved made each day an adventure, and we were thrilled to wake up and know we were going to make art that people enjoyed. We had our three kids and our dog and our dream, and we said, "It is enough."

For several years, our life was exactly that. Enough. We reveled in the experience.

Now, cue the foreboding music and enter the burst of the housing bubble. The reveling turned into reeling.

It's an odd thing when success turns to failure. Life looks a whole lot different when your mind is constantly concerned with questions like how will you pay your bills, how will you afford orthodontia for the kids, and how will you make rice and beans remotely appealing until the next paycheck arrives. *And, really, would living in a tent be so bad?* You forget to notice the sky and the clouds and the way the sunlight sparkles on your daughter's red hair, and you start noticing that every other car is a shiny new BMW and how crowded the fancy restaurants are. At first, you cannot believe your friends are taking carefree family vacations to Cancun, but there's the proof—pictures of them on Facebook, enjoying their prosperity. You forget to walk the dog, although it would do you a world of good to get some exercise, and you eat fast food because it's easy and because slicing up healthy vegetables seems so complicated. You eliminate frivolity and spontaneity, not because you don't have time for them but because those are luxuries rich people enjoy, and you know that "getting away for a weekend" might mean you can't afford supplies for your next project.

Mostly, you wonder why God has let you down, when all you wanted to do was that thing you thought you were created to do. You feel cracks forming in places within your soul that once seemed unshakable. You raise your questions to the sky, but your prayers plummet, seemingly unanswered and ignored.

You feel very alone.

Failure wears like a wet wool coat on a summer day, crushing your frilly party dress of optimism underneath its weight. Survival and existence and going through the motions feel like the best you can do, and sometimes that's all you *can* do. You go to work, you put food on the table, you help with homework, you smile and cheer at your kid's hockey game, you reach for a hand under the blankets at night, and you grasp at every sweet moment you can. But beneath the busyness and activity, you know that something must change—or you will not survive.

This is exactly where I found myself the night the donkey showed up.

Keep in
the heart
of Texas

CHAPTER 1

An Unexpected Guest

Tom hit the brakes and brought our ten-year-old Explorer to an abrupt stop on the gravel. The dust from the tires blew past us and swirled around the animal in our headlights, much like smoke in a stage show.

It was a donkey. In the middle of our driveway.

"What in the world?" my husband muttered as we peered through the windshield at the creature with gigantic ears, caught midchew and looking every bit as surprised as we did. Just twenty feet in front of our bumper, he blinked hard into the bright beams, grass protruding from both sides of his mouth and those unmistakable ears pricked forward. We stared at him as he swallowed his mouthful and stared back at us. Then the ears swiveled around, and he did an about-face, heading for the shadows.

I turned to Tom, my nylon jacket rustling against the seat belt.

"Hey, that's a . . . that's a . . ."

"Donkey," he finished for me. I squeezed my eyes shut, then opened them quickly, just to be sure. Yep, still there. Still a donkey. "What on earth is a donkey doing here?"

Tom leaned forward and squinted through the darkness at the lumpy shape, which now feasted on a clump of early spring grass beyond the headlights. Tom rubbed his chin, assessing the situation. He put the vehicle in "Park" and reached a conclusion before I could say anything else.

"Somebody is going to run into that guy if we don't catch him," he said, almost too tired to get the words out. The narrow, meandering lanes through the Texas countryside, a shadowy March night, speeding locals, and a donkey on the loose . . . it was an accident waiting to happen. And neither an accident nor a donkey roundup was on the list of things we wanted to deal with at the end of a long, hard day.

"Just let him be," I reasoned. "I'm sure someone is out looking for him, and they'll find him and take him home." I watched as the stray donkey plunged his head into another clump, tore off the grass, and munched away. A neighbor's floodlight now illuminated him, and I could see he was scratched up pretty badly. Maybe he'd already been in an accident. He probably did need our help, but still . . . all I could think about was taking a warm shower and crawling into my pajamas. It was well past 9:00 p.m., and we hadn't seen our kids since breakfast. We were exhausted and ready to put this awful day behind us.

I thought back to that morning. It began with the discovery of our client's girdle and brassiere, heaped in a pile on her bathroom floor. Yes, let's start there. The sturdy shapewear was an awkward obstacle right in the middle of the room, hampering our "glamorous" handiwork as we decorated the cramped space with an Italian countryside scene and became intimate friends with the toilet in the process of working around it. Tom finally used a paint stick to scoop up the undergarments, holding them at arm's length and looking away out of gentlemanly respect as he placed them on the tub ledge so he could continue the commode masterpiece. *Good grief, it's hot in here. Why is the thermostat set so high? And why does underwear need so much structure?*

The day ended under the ceiling dome of the home's foyer,

balancing on extension ladders and sweating profusely while we plied our brushes, adding "just a few more details" requested by the client at the last minute to a painting we'd already finished— well beyond the scope of our agreement. Somewhere in between these two events came the horrifying realization that this mural project would not pay the rent.

We were living our dream. Only it had become a nightmare.

Tom and I barely spoke to one another as we loaded up our ladders and artist supplies to head home. Our kids, the two who remained under our roof, had eaten cereal for dinner without us and were hopefully doing something constructive without supervision. I had some reassurance that homework was underway after making several calls from my precarious perch in the foyer, carefully inching the cell phone from my right pocket to my left ear without disturbing my balance. Like every working parent, I wouldn't know for sure until I got home and saw proof.

Grayson, our twelve-year-old son, could be easily distracted by an elaborate Lego project or model airplane, two of his current passions besides ice hockey. Meghan, a senior in high school, might have spent the whole evening on the phone, or writing music for her band, or picking out tomorrow's outfit. Our oldest daughter, Lauren, was in the middle of her first year at a nearby university, studying graphic design and planning a wedding with her high school sweetheart. Between the kids' activities and our workload, life spun like a wobbly top most days. I couldn't help the sigh that escaped my lips.

I pressed my forehead against the cold passenger window in the Explorer and let fatigue wash over me. This wasn't exactly how I'd envisioned our following-the-dream adventure playing out. We had come to the part they don't tell you about in the motivational books and seminars—the part about how in the midst of living out your passion and going for all the marbles, you still need to eat and pay the rent. Life has a way of kicking your dream in the pants. Add to the equation orthodontia for the kids and coming up with college tuition, and you've got something called a painful reality check.

Driving the potholed roads, Tom and I had retreated into our separate worlds of silent defeat and mutual blame. We both needed warm showers and a good night's sleep so we could face our situation with some objectivity in the morning. But as we turned the Ford onto our dirt-and-gravel driveway for the final, dusty quarter mile to our home, there, illuminated by the headlights, was the donkey.

We watched him a few minutes more; then Tom turned off the engine and opened the door. "This won't take long, Rachel," he said over his shoulder. "Stay right there and keep an eye on him, and I'll be right back with a rope to catch him. We'll put him in our pasture tonight and find his owners tomorrow. I don't want to be responsible for anyone getting hurt by running into him with a car."

Obediently, I sat and watched the donkey continue his voracious feast on the roadside grass. *What a pointless animal,* I thought, *but, kind of cute.* As promised, Tom quickly returned with a nylon rope—and a bucket. The donkey, though suspicious of this human stranger, immediately became interested in the contents of the container that Tom shook ever so alluringly, and he stepped closer to inspect it. Oats!

It was then we made the overconfident assumption that "this is gonna be easy."

A classic rookie mistake.

Hey, getting a stray donkey interested in oats is simple. Getting him roped and convincing him to follow is . . . not so much. Tom, a tough outdoorsman with a soft spot for anything in need, seemed to be up for the task in spite of the long day of work he'd had. Cautiously, he closed in on the nervous donkey and gently looped the rope over his gigantic head and around his neck. In a calm voice, Tom urged him to cooperate and flashed a premature thumbs-up at the first tentative steps. See, it *was* going to be easy after all!

"Yay!" I mimed, with a dramatic happy face and my own thumbs-up in reply. I believed the dim moonlight called for some overacting to properly convey my encouragement. Suddenly, the small hooves stopped and dug in. The little guy leaned back and refused to take another step.

Tom coaxed and gave a gentle tug on the rope. The donkey balked.

Tom gave him nibbles of oats. He took two steps forward . . . *yes!* Then five steps to the side . . . *no!* Tom pulled. The donkey pulled harder in the opposite direction. Clearly, this was not working as we had hoped.

Tom called me from the sidelines into active duty. He gave me the rope and went behind the donkey. With a deep breath, Tom pushed. I pulled.

Nothing.

Tom put his shoulder into the animal's rump, braced his feet, and pushed with his legs, while I pulled even harder.

Not an inch. We dropped our hands to our sides and began to strategize.

Tom had a brilliant idea. "Let's switch places," he suggested, but I was not so sure.

"He'd better not have gas!" I moved to the rear and planted my tennis shoes as far away as possible to stay clear of any kicks and possible flatulence, while Tom took hold of the rope at the donkey's head. Still no progress. The animal would not budge. He simply looked at us through heavy-lidded eyes as if to say, "Go ahead, keep trying. This is entertaining." He chewed on the oats like he had all the time in the world.

To our exasperation, all the coaxing, leading, pulling, enticing, and demanding resulted in the donkey only getting farther from our pasture gate than where we had started.

By now, the wind had picked up, and the branches on the trees swayed in an eerie dance that spooked the long-eared intruder. He bolted into a nearby yard, pulling Tom into a run alongside him, my poor husband hanging on to the rope for dear life. A bathrobe-clad neighbor came out to see the ruckus, and she and I stood with our backs to the wind as the cat-and-mouse game continued its spectacle. Three steps forward, two steps back. One step forward, three steps to the side. Cajoling, pushing, pleading, chasing. Mercy, it was hard not to laugh. But when I saw Tom rip the baseball cap off his head and throw it in frustration, I stifled my snicker. His small act of kindness had become a sheer battle of the wills. This. Was. War. Respectfully, I got back into the parked Explorer, pulled a granola bar from my purse, and settled in for the rest of the show.

I watched as they slowly made their way down the blacktop road and back toward our long driveway. A yard lamp back-lit their bodies into black silhouettes, and it was then that I laughed out loud. There was Tom's dark shape, straining hard on the rope until his body practically paralleled the ground. And there stretched the donkey's dark shape, front legs locked, neck drawn forward, and back end sitting down in defiance. It looked just like an old velvet painting I'd once seen of a silhouetted boy and stubborn donkey in the same pose. How I wished I had bought that classic painting for this very moment in time.

Finally Tom found a rhythm the donkey could cooperate with, and the two moved down the driveway, which went across a pond's dam and through a tunnel of swaying trees. With one arm around his opponent's neck while talking quietly into one of those big ears, Tom leaned into the animal and knocked one knee out from under him. As the donkey tried to catch his balance, Tom took advantage of the forward movement and pulled him an extra couple of steps. By fits and starts, the duo arrived at the pasture, and Tom closed the gate on the skinny-rumped creature—three hours later.

"Done!" he said. "I can't wait to get rid of him tomorrow. That was one of the worst experiences of my life! We'll call the county sheriff first thing in the morning."

∧ ∧

By the light of day, Tom and I, along with Meghan and Grayson, gathered in the pasture to take a good look at our unwilling guest.

He was a mess.

Mud and scabs caked his shaggy winter hair into an ugly, matted coat. Fresh gashes from barbed wire fences seemed to be everywhere, from head to hoof, oozing and bleeding. The scratches crisscrossed his face and legs, with a four-inch slice that went deep into the flesh of his barrel chest. The wounds needed immediate attention, so we cleaned and dressed them with ointment as the donkey trembled inside our three-sided barn. Although it seemed as if he knew our efforts were meant to help him, he allowed only brief touches before skittishly moving just beyond our reach. His lips quivered, and his tail swished nervously. We moved in slow motion, using hushed voices as we worked.

"It's okay, donkey. You're okay," we reassured him. What else had he experienced before his sudden arrival here? We wondered aloud about his past.

Under the mud, he was a light brownish-gray color, with a white muzzle that looked as if it had been dipped in a deep bucket of buttermilk. A matching creamy-white color circled his big brown eyes and covered the underside of his belly with soft hair. With faint stripes adorning sturdy legs, he stood no taller than four feet at the shoulder. *How can an animal this compact be so difficult to manage?* The daylight made him seem so . . . well, compliant.

A wispy mane trickled down a broad neck, and his tail, unlike a horse's, was a strong shaft of muscle and bone with long strands of coarse hair starting partway down. A long, dark stripe down the center of his back began at his mane and disappeared into his tail. Up close, his ears were even bigger than I'd remembered from the night before. Thick and mobile, they were never pointing the same direction for very long. The caramel-colored fuzz that covered them was outlined by dark hair around the edges and tufted with cream on the insides. His straight black eyelashes made his eyes seem a little sad, or maybe it was just the way his large head drooped that gave him such a melancholy air.

"Oh look!" Grayson pointed out in delight from his perch on the fence. "He has a cross on his back!" A chocolate-brown pattern of hair emblazoned across his shoulders distinctly intersected the dark stripe down his back. Legend has it that every donkey bears the symbol of Christ, in honor of His triumphant entry into Jerusalem before His crucifixion. Seeing a donkey face-to-face for the first time certainly brought the biblical story to mind. Our eyes lingered on this marking and then wandered to his many wounds. He was, as we say in Texas, "tore up."

Tom put his arm across Grayson's shoulders as we made our way through the tall grass back to the house, while Meghan stayed to keep the donkey company. A creature lover since she was a toddler, Meghan once claimed the ability to talk to animals. Although this one was much larger than the hamsters and parakeets she'd communicated with before, he still looked as if he needed a friend.

She sat on a wooden step in the barn near the shy donkey, chin in hand, and listened to the birds sing in the rafters as she watched him. With wary eyes on her, the donkey kept his distance but lingered in the barn, rather than making for the pasture beyond. After some minutes had ticked by, he took one hesitant step toward the slim, redheaded girl, then paused as if thinking.

Then another step. A little closer.

A fly buzzed.

"It's okay, buddy," Meghan murmured. She turned a palm up in silent beckoning.

And another step.

A long minute. Ears twitching. Blowing hard. The chirping birds oblivious to the slow dance below.

"I won't hurt you."

Closer.

"You're safe now."

A little closer still . . . until his tentative nostrils touched her knees.

"It's all right."

He sniffed her scent and paused again. His long ears turned forward. Tail swished the fly. Finally, he closed his eyes and took one last step, resting his giant head in her lap with a deep donkey sigh. Meghan's hand came up and gently stroked his face and ears. She scratched his neck and whispered softly to him. His lower lip sagged sleepily as he relaxed for the first time since his arrival. The donkey and girl stayed just so for a long while, his head heavy on her legs as she caressed him and gently untangled his scraggly mane.

I was in the kitchen when Meghan came bursting through the door. "Oh Momma! He's *sweet!*" she exclaimed as she described the quiet moments in the barn. She finished with a breathless, "Can we keep him, pleeze??"

Drying my hands on a towel, I looked at her pleading expression. I should have known this was coming. *Here we go. Don't you start begging for a donkey.* Sweet or not, we knew he had to belong to someone. Surely. I mean, how can a person misplace a donkey, for heaven's sake? His owners *must* be looking for him.

"Meggie, you can't let yourself get attached to him. You know he's not going to be here long." I smoothed the disappointment from her forehead and continued. "He's going to be on his way just as soon as we find out where he belongs, and I don't want you to get your heart broken when he leaves."

"But what if nobody claims him?" she appealed. "Then can we keep him?"

"Honey, I don't think we are 'donkey people.' We don't know

the first thing about them. We certainly don't have any use for one. And besides, I think you're getting ahead of yourself. We need to do what we can to find his home before we start making any plans." But in my mind, I'd already been wondering the same thing.

Just then, we heard noise from outside, near the pasture gate. We hurried to see what the fuss was about and found our yellow Lab, Beau, wagging his entire body as he barked and whined in excitement. A new friend! He could hardly contain his joy. The donkey, who had left the barn and ventured toward the house, looked up in surprise.

"Beau is anxious to say hello," Grayson said as he came from around the corner and attempted to grab Beau's collar to calm him. But the one-hundred-pound dog had already squeezed his slobbery self under the gate and loped across the open space to where the donkey stood, frozen in alarm. Beau's hefty tail worked from side to side as he approached the donkey with shameless curiosity and wiggly welcome.

For a split second the donkey held still, taking him in. Then, like a bolt of lightning, he whirled around and struck out with his back left hoof. Yelping in shock, Beau came to an abrupt skid on his haunches. The donkey turned and lowered his head, breathing heavily, while Beau backed up and let out a whimper. The two locked eyes as they circled one another. Donkey: ears flat, head low, nostrils flared. Dog: ears forward, hair raised, nose twitching. The hoof had missed Beau's chest, but the message it delivered was clear: Stay away. Rebuffed, the dog finally returned to the gate, looking over his shoulder with his tail tucked and eyes filled with confusion. Poor Beau. He'd never been rejected so soundly in his whole life!

"Beau needs to learn to slow down a little," I said as we huddled over the dog to comfort him. I looked back to see the donkey, still breathing hard and agitated. "He scared the poor guy half to death with all that energy!" Too much, too soon.

∧ ∧

That week, we went into action. We posted signs, contacted authorities, and checked with local feed stores. We looked for the donkey's owner high and low. But no one seemed to be missing a donkey. It was like he appeared out of thin air. Onto our property. Like a rabbit out of a hat.

When the county sheriff stopped by our house, we learned that our situation was far from unique: People simply abandoned their donkeys along country roads when they tired of caring for them, given that the animals have life spans of thirty or forty years. Droughts always bring high numbers of strays, and we were in the middle of a bad one. Many people can't afford to keep these cute-but-grass-consuming animals who compete for grazing land with cattle, so they dump them off. Without so much as a second thought.

"Yep, novelty wears off real quick," the sheriff said in his Texas drawl. "Ya see a lotta sad cases out here." He adjusted his wide-brimmed hat and looked at the donkey. "Now, this fella here is young. He's not even a mature male, if you know what I mean." He cleared his throat as we digested the meaning of "mature male" and glanced underneath his thin belly to see what the sheriff was talking about. Aah, yes.

The lawman's thick mustache twitched as he continued. "It's pretty typical to see males let loose like this. You don't see the females as often because they're better at keeping coyotes away from cattle and goats, but these jacks . . . well, I can't even get five dollars for 'em at auction. Nobody wants 'em. Basically, they're worthless animals."

"But what happens to them if no one takes them from your auction?" I asked, not wanting to know the answer.

He paused for a moment. "We try to find a rescue organization that will take 'em. There are some reputable ones around, and they do a good job taking these guys off our hands. Problem is, right now, they're filled up over their capacity, and it's tough to place these new strays. Ya hate to think what could happen, but the reality is the state can't afford to keep feeding 'em indefinitely."

The donkey's ears twitched toward us, as if eavesdropping on the discussion of his fate.

Horrified that he might have overheard, I looked at Tom for support and suggested, "How about if we just keep him here until his owners contact your office?" Tom nodded in agreement, and the sheriff beamed.

"Sounds good. Real good. Now, I've got three other jacks in my custody . . ." He trailed off, bushy eyebrows raised in an unspoken question.

Tom hurriedly thanked him for his time and said we'd look forward to his call. We parted ways before this whole rescue thing got even more out of hand.

^ ^

The weeks stretched on, and Lauren, our oldest redhead, came home from college to finish planning her wedding to Robert. It was just a couple of months away, and we had some work to do in order to pull it off. With the five of us all together, we felt like a complete circle once again, a little family staying afloat on a swift river of painting projects and dress fittings. Somehow we limped through the financial disaster that had loomed the night the donkey showed up, and we were managing to barter, trade, and "do it yourself" through the wedding details. Our problems were far from solved, but we did our best to pretend they didn't exist. At least for now.

A warm stillness hung in the air as we gathered at the fence to look at this wounded, and apparently worthless, stray who had given rescue such a fight. His sores had not yet healed, but he looked remarkably good in spite of the two permanent scars across his nose. Already his thin stomach was filling out, and his patchy hair, without all the burrs and scabs, felt soft under our touch.

There had been no response whatsoever to our search for his owner, and we knew a decision needed to be made. We could turn him over to the county and some unknown future, or we could provide a home for him, at least for now. Obviously, the three kids and I would launch an all-out campaign to keep him.

"Look at him out there. He *is* pretty sweet," we pointed out. He nibbled daintily on the green blades of grass and swatted flies with that funny tail of his. He seemed . . . perfectly innocuous. Charming, even.

Tom was having none of this "permanence" thing, and it seemed he had Beau on his side. "I've seen the dark side of him," he rebutted, remembering that first night. "He's impossible to handle, and he's stubborn and obviously not very bright. And Beau hates him—don't you, Beau?" At that, the donkey looked up and gave a snort. He shook his long ears so they flapped together in a kind of ear-clap as if he were replying, "Hey, now! I heard that."

Beau barked in return. He didn't exactly *hate* the donkey after their first encounter. However, the donkey seemed to hate *him*. They weren't any closer to friendship, and in fact, they appeared to be in an animal standoff. But I had faith. After all, *no one* can hate a good yellow Lab. And who could resist such an adorable donkey? I was sure they just needed time to bond. Perhaps Beau could learn to be less extroverted, giving the donkey a chance to see beyond the teeth and tail to the warm heart that was just a *bit* overeager. Their relationship would take some work.

The kids picked up the lobbying. "Dad, we Googled 'donkey care' and found out that donkeys are pretty low maintenance. They don't need expensive food, they don't require extra special care, and all they really need is shelter in bad weather. Which we already have." They pointed to the barn, unused except for storage.

"Yeah, well, I'm pretty sure it's not as simple as that. It never is. I think a little more research is in order, guys. We just don't need another mouth to feed," Tom volleyed, mindful of our precarious bank balance. "Think of the vet bills and hay. I mean, look at him out there. He's a pig. He's going to require a lot of food at the rate he's going." Then he pulled out the reasoning every parent gives to every child at some point in their lives: "You kids can't remember to feed the dog, much less a donkey, so don't expect *me* to take care of him for you. We're not keeping him, period."

Tom did have a point about not remembering to feed the dog; they couldn't argue that. But of course they insisted that this would be completely different. Despite his tough talk, I'd seen Tom out there trying to befriend the scruffy donkey when he thought no one was looking. Day after day, he sat on a camp chair in the middle of the pasture for long periods of time. He brought a book to read, or watched the birds, or looked at some imaginary point in the distance, in hopes that the donkey would simply become comfortable in his presence. It was as if Tom instinctively knew (unlike Beau) to leave the pace of trust up to the donkey.

At first, the donkey had given the man in the chair a wide berth, grazing in a perimeter far beyond his reach. He shied back from any sudden movement of Tom's arms. Every now and then he'd look over at Tom, all the while chewing, taking him in, assessing.

Had the donkey been mistreated at the hands of a man in previous encounters? If only he could tell us. I could see that the donkey's resistance to our rescue had been rooted in some kind of fear, and it broke my heart to think that someone could hurt such a sweet animal.

Gradually, the donkey's self-designated perimeter around Tom's chair grew smaller. He inched nearer. And one afternoon, as Tom read his book, he heard the grass rustle behind him. He felt a nose on his shoulder. A sniff on his neck. Lips gently nibbling his collar.

"Hey, Donkey Boy." Tom's voice was soft, calm. "That's a good boy. That's a good boy."

He slowly lifted his hand and cupped the donkey's head. The wall began to crumble.

Brave enough now to come near for a carrot and gentle petting, he still seemed so vulnerable. And was it me, or did his soft brown eyes seem slightly hopeful? Perhaps I was projecting.

"What do the neighbors think about his braying?" Lauren asked, breaking a twig off the tree by the fence. "I actually heard

him from way down the road the other day! Sounded like someone was being killed over here."

Right on cue, the donkey lifted his head and began heaving
his sides. His lips pulled back to reveal a big set of teeth as a
foghorn-like sound exploded from his mouth. *HEE-haw, HEE-
haw, HEE-haw, haw, haw.* I suppose it could be disturbing if
you weren't used to it, but in truth, I loved hearing his bray
because it reminded me of growing up in Mexico as a missionary kid. We'd lived there off and on during my growing-up
years. Burros were everywhere, carrying loads of sticks, pulling
carts, and posing in their colorful, fringed halters with tour-
ists. I thought they were such beautiful creatures, and I'd try
to imitate their brays as we drove past, sticking my head out
the car window and letting out a *HEE-haw!* in what I thought
was a friendly overture. Not one of them ever seemed remotely
impressed, but that didn't keep me from trying.

As the donkey's bray subsided, we considered the pros and
cons of keeping him.

"We probably wouldn't ride him, like we would a real horse,
would we?" asked Grayson.

"I guess you *could*, but it seems like it would be a really slow
ride," Tom replied. "Plus, we'd have to train him, and we don't
know anything about that."

True, true. Nods all around.

"What if we put him to work around here?" Meghan offered.
"We could plant a big garden, and he could pull a plow."

We thought about that for a minute.

"Nah. That would never happen."

"Too bad we don't have a mine," I laughed. "He could haul
wagonloads of gold, and we could all be rich."

Our chuckles subsided, and I could see that Tom was just one good reason away from letting him stay. Think, family, think.

"Well, he's fun to look at," said Grayson, glancing up at his dad.

"Yes! Yes, he is!" we chimed in. "Very fun to look at! And nice to talk about!"

"You mean he's a conversation piece?" Tom's voice had softened with his smile at the thought.

"Yeah, like what if we had some weird relatives from the city over, and we didn't have anything to talk about? We could always just bring them out here to see the donkey, and they'd probably love it." Grayson was making a solid case here. Just needed one final push . . .

"I bet we could get ten minutes of conversation out of it," Lauren said in support. "Possibly fifteen. People would find him really interesting." Four pairs of eyes turned toward Tom with laser-like focus.

"Ah, excellent point. I guess you could say he makes good yard art," Tom conceded as he opened the gate and stepped close to the donkey. Still moving slowly around him, Tom reached forward to rub the insides of his ears. I felt in my pocket for the carrot slice that I'd brought from the kitchen.

"Listen, you guys." He took a breath. "We can keep him if . . ."

The cheers from the group nearly drowned the provisional addendum he was about to tack on.

"Ahem!" Tom regained our attention by quashing our congratulatory noise with his hand motions. "As I was saying, we can keep him . . . *if* he is indeed as low maintenance as you say he will be, *if* he does not eat too much, and *if* he is an upstanding citizen around here."

Simple! Piece of cake! We've got this! We went back to

cheering, and naturally, our exuberance spooked the donkey in question. With a toss of his head, and hind legs bucking, he spun around and trotted for the far corner of the pasture, but not before snatching the carrot from my hand in a greedy chomp.

Beau barked his opposition to the arrangement, possibly the last voice of reason.

Something told me this was not going to be as simple as I thought.

CHAPTER 2
What's in a Name?

The donkey's temporary citizenship gave both Tom and me a mental reprieve from our worries. And it helped me avoid the feeling of defeat that had settled in my stomach, like a wad of cookie dough, which is always a huge mistake to eat in the first place. Watching our new resident become familiar with his home, and learn to trust us in the process, provided a relief valve, not to mention a favorite topic of dinner conversation.

"Hey, have you noticed how the donkey can reach almost every part of his body with his teeth, to scratch wherever he itches? Pass the butter, please."

"I know! I saw him reach underneath his tail today. He bent completely in half, backward, flipped up his tail, and started scratching it! Rolls, anyone?"

"Seriously, I think he is double-jointed or something. More spaghetti, thank you."

We quickly learned to watch his velvety ears, which moved constantly. Pricked forward showed his interest and inquisitive nature. Facing backward meant he was afraid, uncertain, displeased. One forward and one back . . . well, it called for interpretation, especially when accompanied by a hoof stomp or tail swish. His ears were a key part of his communication—a silent form of expression that delighted us.

We began to educate ourselves about donkey care: what kind of diet was best, how to groom him, how to care for his hooves, which vaccines he'd need. Our pasture, labeled "unimproved" by the county, was perfect for this animal who was made for arid desert life. The tough native grasses in our six-acre pasture, baked by the Texas sun and blown by incessant winds, would provide enough nutritional roughage without being too rich. The back section of the fenced area included woods that he could use for shade and foraging. He would need little supplemental feed, except perhaps in winter months, or in the peak of summer scorchers, when grass withered to brown dust. There was more to learn than we thought, but the donkey's gentle temperament invited our attention and affection.

Since he had worked his way into our barn and our hearts, we knew it was time to give him a real name. In our family's history, we'd ceremoniously christened a succession of pets: Checkers, the springer spaniel with brown and white markings; Buttons and Twix, handsome cat brothers; Wilson, the parakeet we rescued when we found him bouncing across the street like a tennis ball. And there was Angel, the red-tailed hawk Tom once had when he practiced falconry. Even the gerbils and fish had fancy names bestowed upon them during their brief lives in our care.

The challenge had always been to find a moniker that would fit each animal's personality, yet wouldn't cause embarrassment if we had to yell the name in public. Over the years, Tom, on the grounds of his manhood, vetoed cutesy names like "Schmoozy," "Fluffy," and "Snookums" for our family menagerie, and we agreed it was a reasonable enough guideline to follow. You shouldn't make a guy who's most comfortable in camouflage have a pet whose name suggests it should be carried inside a pink purse.

"So what do you think we should call him?" I asked Tom,

whose reflection I caught in the mirror while I did double duty—brushing my teeth and inspecting the crow's-feet around my eyes. "Should we go with something comical since he is, after all, a *donkey* for crying out loud? Or should we find something sort of stately?" We had never had much trouble deciding with our other pets, but for whatever reason, this was quite the dilemma.

Tom sat on the bed and put on his work shoes. "Not to confuse things, but since we live in Texas, there's also an abundance of Spanish names we could consider."

"That's true!" He knew how much I loved those burros from my childhood. This was getting more complicated by the minute.

We spent some time tossing around various ideas but decided to keep thinking as we went on with our day.

While up on scaffolding, we moved on to the silly: Brae, Harry, Eeyore.

"Having a donkey is fun, but he's not something I want to make fun of," Tom objected, dipping his brush into blue paint and wiping the excess on the rim of the can. We crossed those names off our list.

The business of naming him came up at all hours of the day. In the evening, over a mass of open *Bride* magazines and popcorn, the girls suggested something more serious, more dignified. "What about Jefferson, or Winston? Henry? Roosevelt?" Better, but still not right.

Maybe some biblical inspiration? At bedtime, we considered Balaam; Ichabod; and Jonah, Micah, and all the other minor prophets.

No matter what we tried, nothing seemed to fit. He was the Nameless Braying One of the Pasture, and it bothered us. The weeks drifted by with no solution.

"We can't just keep calling him 'Donkey Boy,'" I said as Tom and I unloaded ladders into the barn one afternoon. "It seems a little impersonal, and just slightly like we don't care." We stopped to watch him mosey along, enjoying the sunshine, his hooves dragging from one end of the field to the other.

"I know. But the right name is important. You don't want to mess that up, even for a donkey that we couldn't get five dollars for." Tom winked and threw an arm over my shoulder, then quickly removed it in the sticky heat. "You know," he reflected, "that guy is never in a hurry. It's like he's in a time warp. He could never get anywhere in a flash."

We looked at each other, and the light dawned. *Flash!* That was it!

Flash. As in a speeding superhero who comes to the rescue of one in distress. We chuckled at the thought of our new donkey in a mask emblazoned with lightning bolts, stopping to take a nap en route to thwarting a crisis. Yes, it was perfect. The kids approved.

As soon as Flash was named, we knew without saying that his probation had ended and he could now be considered a bona fide member of the family. We walked right into it, eyes wide open.

Here's a piece of advice that comes free with this book: Rescuer, beware. As soon as you name a stray animal, it's *yours*. For better or for worse. Yours, baby. You need to think about that the next time you pick up a stray kitty and start calling her "Pookie" while you're trying to find a home for her. Face it—Pookie is yours, and she became yours the minute you pronounced those two syllables.

Flash was ours for keeps, and we fell in love with him. He

shed his shaggy winter hair, revealing a smooth, gray-brown coat that made him look positively sleek. Even his ears lost most of their wool and became silky soft, especially at their base near the knob on the top of his head. He loved having the insides of these long, tubular appendages rubbed and looked forward to any attention that came his way.

Being groomed became his favorite pastime, and I used it as a bonding opportunity, talking to him as I worked the brush over his body. He seemed interested in my chatter, so I filled him in on our projects, kept him abreast of our family activities, and told him whatever came to my mind. His ears followed my voice, turning this way and that, and he'd nod every now and then, suggesting his response: "Go on, tell me more." I quickly realized he was the perfect listener, the kind who makes you feel he has all the time in the world for your story. Whenever the currycomb came out, he relaxed into a puddle of equine bliss. You could almost see him smile. Flash's shyness slowly melted away, and we began to see glimpses of an outgoing personality.

Flash made himself at home at our place. Our yellow, 1970s barn-shaped house, properly deemed "gambrel style," sat next to his new pasture and gave us a prime view of his activities. He had it made: an abundance of wide-open space to aimlessly wander under a big sky, a barn for shelter, and two acres of shady woods to explore.

Four years earlier, when we had found the property through an ad in the paper, we had no use for most of it, except to store supplies in the empty barn. We gladly abandoned our suburban life and set about making the rented fixer-upper our home— on a dime, of course. Though just twenty miles outside of the Dallas metroplex, it felt like a world away from the city.

The quarter-mile driveway wound atop a dam, past a pond, and through some woods before coming around to the house in a clearing. The "charming farmhouse" (as described in the paper) contained some strange features, such as a toilet crammed so close to the wall that it required sidesaddle positioning and a sense of humor to make it work. But once we replaced the carpet and painted the antiseptic, white semigloss walls and ceilings with pleasant new colors, it felt like a real home.

The kids' bedrooms were nestled under the sloping eaves of the barnlike roof and had dormer window seats—perfect spots for daydreaming, which we encouraged. Though tiny, the kitchen had plenty of faux wood countertops and enough cabinet space for all our cookware. As I washed dishes, I could look out the window to an ever-changing view of grasses and wildflowers in a field that sloped down to a wooded creek bed.

Mighty bur oaks, red oaks, and cedars filled the woods and transformed with the seasons, providing an endless array of beauty. *We've been starved for this.* We soaked it in. Granted, the septic system backed up regularly, and almost every fixture needed replacing. But those were small hindrances. Our family could breathe here, and the eighteen acres of land that came with the house was more than we could have hoped for. It became our sanctuary in the midst of our tightrope walk of financial insecurity. We had no money, but the view was priceless.

With his calm presence gracing the property, Flash seemed to complete our new lifestyle. It just felt right to have hay bales on hand for our "livestock," to check fences for needed repairs, and to pet an eager nose over the gate. Even Beau seemed to resign himself to sharing our affection with another animal, although he made a point to bark at Flash whenever he could.

∧ ∧

We had only had Flash for a couple of months when our landlords stopped by to visit. They'd just moved into an old cottage that was on the same property we rented from them, which now made us neighbors. A Louisiana–born-and-bred blonde belle, Bridgette made a striking contrast to her husband, Steve, a tall, bearded Midwesterner. Where Bridgette was vivacious and talkative, Steve was reserved and quiet. While Steve favored flannel shirts and jeans, Bridgette always looked as if she'd stepped out of a fashion magazine, her athletic figure accentuated by slim skirts and fitted blouses. Bridgette had pioneered a prestigious architectural design firm in Dallas and represented everything I was not: beautiful, educated, confident, successful, worldly, fit, stylish, professional. I avoided her as often as possible. Which was not easy, since they now neighbored us.

Bridgette and Steve had recently married and shed their fabulous careers and chic downtown Dallas loft to strike out on their own as entrepreneurs. Everything about them was cool—even the fact they had downsized to the small house on the property. They designed corporate spaces from their front porch by day and worked in their organic garden in the evenings. I'm quite sure they loved hummus and knew all about fine wines.

Beneath the shade of the cedar trees that lined the pasture, we chitchatted about the weather and caught up on the neighborhood news. Just then, Flash meandered up to the gate, looking for an ear scratch.

"Have you met our new donkey?" I asked, turning to see if they were impressed.

"Oh, we've already made friends with this guy," Bridgette drawled as she reached forward, her expensive bracelets clanking. "Idn't he jus' *ado*rable! We jus' *love* him."

We smiled like proud new parents, pleased with their progeny. Yes, Flash was a real member of the family. A keeper. We started to gush about his emerging qualities, but what we heard next silenced the words on our lips.

"And guess what!" Bridgette continued, enthusiasm spilling. "We've given him the *perfect* name!"

Our smiles froze in place. *Wait. You've done what?*

She paused dramatically as we stared, wide-eyed in disbelief. With a flourish, she went for the Big Reveal. "His name is . . . *Hay*-soos! You know, it's a Spaynish name!" She clapped her hands together in delight. "Idn't that *per*fect?"

Perfect? No, not in the least. *Jesús*, while a common name in Spanish, would never be used for *my* donkey, who already had a name: *Flash*.

"Well, *hi*, *Hay*-soos! How ya doin'?" she greeted Flash as he nosed in for more affection. She pronounced "hi" like "hah," and it suddenly grated on my nerves. Flash clearly did not share my misgivings about this name because he homed right in on the attention.

So pleased with their excellent naming of *our* animal, these well-meaning neighbors seemed oblivious to our awkward protest that he'd already been named Flash. By us. His owners. The people he belongs to. The ones who own him. *Yeah.* Nope, they just kept talking.

"*Hay*-soos is so entertaining! We just love giving him carrots over the fence and tickling those big ol' lips of his!" They laughed, throwing their heads back in delight. But all we could hear was "*Hay*-soos this" and "*Hay*-soos that," and each time, we became more annoyed.

The nerve. To name someone else's pet. Why, I'd never dream of going over to their house and presuming to rename one of their fancy cats. My back prickled.

^ ^

I heard Miss Southern Belle, Bridgette, calling Flash from her backyard. "*Yoo-hoo!* Hah, *Hay*-soos! Come heah, darlin!" she cooed. I closed my eyes and clenched my teeth.

"Don't go, Flash. Don't go over there. Don't answer to that!" I sent thought waves to encapsulate my new donkey in a protective mental force field, willing him to stay away.

But no. Uh-uh. Flash appeared to be completely over his initial shyness as he trotted over to the fence, happy as a clam to respond to his alias—especially if there were carrots involved. Day after day, I watched in disgust as he sold his dignity for a handout. *Flash, where is your self-respect?*

This could mean only one thing: war. A subtle war. I hitched up my mom jeans and applied some lipstick. A shot of hair spray. Ready.

I dropped Flash's name into every conversation with our neighbors, whether it fit the context or not.

"Nice weather we're having! *Flash* sure is enjoying it." I emphasized his name with just a little edge and waited for their response, which never came.

"Oh, what a lovely outfit you're wearing. I should call *Flash* over here to admire it."

"I hear there's a new movie coming out. I sure wish I could take *Flash* to see it."

I made a point of correcting every mention of the unmentionable name I heard. But, having been raised in church, I did it only in the nicest, sweetest way possible, so as to keep my Christian witness.

Bridgette said, "I just loove to heah *Hay*-soos bray! He just makes me happy."

"Oh, I know." I smiled. "*Flash* can certainly make some noise. *Flash* is so silly. *Flash* really likes to hear himself." My strategy seemed to fall on deaf ears.

Undaunted, I employed another tactic: I spoke directly to Flash himself. He obviously needed a good talking-to so he would stop running over to Bridgette every time she called him by that other name. Not his real name. The name that somebody else dubbed him.

I took my donkey's shaggy head into my hands and looked into his warm, brown eyes. He flared his nostrils and gave me an innocent look in return. His muzzle hairs poked in all directions, giving him an extra boost of audaciousness.

"Flash," I said. "Baby, you've got to stop this business of responding to '*Hay*-soos' every time you hear it, when *that is not your name.* You already have a name: Flash. It's Flash, because I own you, and I'm the only one who has the right to name you. Other people can *call* you any other name in the book, but get this straight: That's not your name. You belong to me. You are *mine.* Therefore, whatever name I've given you—that's your name."

I saw a spark of understanding in his expression, so I let him go. But not without one last mom glare and a two-finger point from my eyes to his and back again that told him I meant business. I wanted to see a change in his behavior, and that was that. He lowered his head and kicked the dirt. Yes, he obviously understood.

Now if I could only get over feeling intimidated by our wildly successful neighbors and flat out *tell* Bridgette and Steve to knock it off. But I somehow couldn't bring myself to confront them. I felt fine with light, brief conversation and thinly veiled hints, but I'd seen Bridgette's website with her impressive bio, the list of prestigious boards she served on, and the glossy photographs of all her high-end corporate architectural designs . . . and the words just stuck in my throat. My paint-splattered work clothes, the Ford Explorer with fading paint, and the postdated rent check only reinforced that they were way out of our league. *Ugh.*

In truth, this little spat over Flash's name had brought up insecurities I'd been trying to squelch. The change in our location and scenery hadn't changed the fact that I was coming up short on all fronts and that my failures kept bubbling over, no matter how hard I tried to keep a lid on them. The razor-thin edge of the will-we-or-won't-we-make-it pursuit of our artistic dreams seemed to amplify my shortcomings. Being confronted with a gorgeous couple who seemed to have it all only made my flaws all the more obvious.

But I couldn't think about that now. I needed to paint a princess-themed nursery for a client, and I hadn't quite figured out how I was going to get it done in the time I'd allotted. I rushed to sketch the design on the wall and quickly lost myself in the work.

"Mom, did you forget to pick me up?" Grayson's voice on my cell phone brought me scrambling down my ladder at the job site and hurrying to the truck in a fit of panic. How could it be 4:30 already? He'd been waiting an hour for me.

"I'll be right there, Gray. I'm so sorry! I forgot about the time."

How could I have been so thoughtless? It was Grayson's first day of middle school; I'd vowed that on this day I would start doing a better job of staying organized, and I'd already failed.

"Stupid, stupid, stupid!" I chided myself as I sped the seventy miles from the job site to his school. "I am so stupid!" I arrived an hour later to find him sitting in the darkened school office, a secretary keeping him company as the poor kid waited for his negligent mom to come. *Happy first day of sixth grade, son. Mommy loves you. She just forgot about you.*

My failures as a mother stacked up relentlessly. I remembered how I used to have a nice dinner on the table at a decent time, and how I kept the house picked up and tended our children's needs with focus and energy. These days, keeping our heads above water meant putting in long work hours. Loading ladders and equipment each day exhausted me, and my evening hours were spent planning and sketching upcoming projects.

On the one hand, I enjoyed the work and loved the creativity, but I was a distracted parent, and one with a short temper, at best. I missed the simpler days, when my goals as a mother had been clear and I had the time to be intentional in my parenting. I hated pulling shirts from the bottom of the clothes hamper and fluffing them in the dryer with antistatic sheets, trying to pass them off as clean. This system fooled nobody. Chipping frozen ground beef in the frying pan while my hungry family gnawed on chips at 8:00 p.m. demoralized me. Bedtime devotions with the kids? Ha.

"*Inadequate.*" I dug the word into my journal with my pen, tearing the pages with the force. My distractedness, my inability to complete a task, my failure to see the things that were important to my husband—it was a recurring theme in our marriage when things got tough.

We are fortunate; our conflicts are few and far between. But when we have them, it seems they center on differences in priorities, and I take it hard. He's the planner, while I work off of a hope and a prayer. He's the one who measures to the centimeter, while I eyeball and guess. He needs things tidy, and I don't see the mess. When you're the "close-is-good-enough" partner to a "do-it-right-or-not-at-all" person, it's easy to feel like the biggest failure-wife of all time. It wasn't Tom's fault I took things that way. . . . It was mine. I'd hear him make a small request for, say, remembering to buy toothpaste, and I'd naturally assume it meant I was completely inadequate and worthless.

My focus got lost. *I* got lost. Yes, the Texas landscape was beautiful, but I couldn't see it anymore. My to-do list overwhelmed me. Everything clamored for attention: The laundry needed sorting; Grayson needed help with a science project; our new client waited on a sketch; weeds overtook the flower beds; we were out of milk; the Explorer's engine made knocking sounds; hockey practice started in an hour. . . . I imploded. I'd begin one task, only to be pulled by another, then another, and at the end of the day have nothing done.

There were some mornings when I couldn't even get out of bed, let alone wage war over my donkey's name.

Just then I heard Bridgette's cheery greeting to Flash ring out yet again. I sighed. And as I peered through the curtain to see him eagerly trotting to the fence with his ears wobbling from side to side, something strange happened. I felt a whisper. Okay, maybe not even a whisper, but *something*. A nudge, a thought. A tickle on my skin.

Snippets from a verse dropped into my head:

I have called you by name; you are mine.

The words caught me off guard. Where had I heard them before? *I know I've read them somewhere.* I reached for my Bible and flipped pages, finally finding them in Isaiah 43:1:

But now, O Jacob, listen to the LORD who created you.
O Israel, the one who formed you says,
"Do not be afraid, for I have ransomed you.
I have called you by name; you are mine."

The letters leaped off the page.
"You are mine."
Deep breath. Oh. I had not expected this. As much as I believed in a God who cared about me and could certainly speak to anyone, at any time, I wondered if this might be that "still small voice" that people talked about. Consumed by my little vortex of failure, I'd been doing more blaming than connecting with Him. I just kept muddling, struggling, failing, and repeating.

But somehow, He was using a donkey to lead me to a simple truth.

How apropos.

Because I felt pretty much like a donkey's hind end. I was no different from Flash. I had an identity crisis of my own going on. Somehow, in the busyness of the kids' activities, work, cooking, paying the bills, and trying to juggle it all, I'd stopped paying attention to my spiritual life. Prayer had become little more than accusations and pleas for help, addressed to a God somewhere up there. Time spent listening for Him, or reading His Word, was nonexistent. *Why bother?* Focusing on myself, *my* problems, and *my* solutions, I had let the connection with my Maker go cold.

I saw myself as the center of my own universe, utterly inadequate in everything. Dropping all the balls. A failure in my artistic venture. A terrible businesswoman. A mom who forgot to pick up her kid at school. Alone, even in the middle of a beautiful family. Lost, in the midst of a new country life. Always behind, forever floundering. Afraid of being discovered as a fraud. *Who am I kidding? I'm nobody.* I listened to the whispers that called into question my value—value that was based on my performance instead of the magnificent grace poured out on me from the heart of a loving heavenly Father.

The One whose I am. The One who named me.

I'd forgotten just who I belonged to, and that my Father had given me a name—in fact, many names—that expressed His love for me. In that moment, God reminded me that my value comes from my relationship with Him, and not my "success" as a mom, or as a wife, or as a friend, or as a businessperson.

I grabbed a small spiral notebook and wrote,

Remember your name.

Below it I put these words:

Know who you belong to.

Then I realized that, like a good Texan with poor grammar, something about that sentence wasn't right. We'd say it, "Know who ya belong ta." So I scribbled it out and carefully printed,

Know whose you are.

Know whose you are. I paused and looked out the window. *My identity really starts and ends with the One who created me.* There is a beautiful poem in Psalm 139 that says He knit us together in the womb and knows our innermost parts. He created us in His image and then sat back and said, "It is good." Blinking hard, I realized something: God doesn't make mistakes. He created me to be uniquely me, and I had simply forgotten *whose* I was. I had been operating from the wrong owner's manual.

Oh boy. As my own master, the names I called myself. Names I responded to as soon as I heard them. Names that weren't actually mine.

Failure.
Worthless.
Inadequate.
Afraid.
Fraud.
Stupid.

I wrote the names in my notebook and continued listing every name I could think of that I called myself. In the end, I had a pretty long and pathetic list. On so many levels I had beat myself up in my "self-talk." Forgetting who I belonged to had created an open season for blasting away at myself. And I suddenly realized that I'd let my very *identity* be formed by the names I called myself, because I had confused what I do *with who I am.* I saw myself through a distorted prism. All I had to do was think back to my last low moment, and bingo—I could

hear myself saying, "Hello, My Name Is _____."
Just as if I were wearing it on a name tag.

Hello, My Name Is _____:
Afraid: I'm paralyzed by fear of rejection and failure.
Alone: No one understands me.
Unloved: If God loved me, how could He allow this?
Unlovable: I'm obviously not worth loving.
Lost: I will never find my way.
Unworthy: I cannot accept love and affirmation because
    I'm such a loser.
Failure: Um, obvious.
Sinner: I keep committing the same stupid sins over
    and over again.
Damaged: My wounds are too deep to heal.
Ugly: God used all His best stuff on the cheerleaders
    and gave me the leftovers.
Defeated: Why even try?
Stupid: I am constantly making dumb mistakes.
Fake: One day everyone will find out I'm not who they
    think I am.
Inadequate: I cannot measure up to the woman I should
    be for the people I love.
Nobody: I don't matter.

That afternoon, it hit me. As a child of God, I belong to
Him. He made me. He owns me. I am His.
This. Changes. Everything.
God sees me through the lens of eternity, through grace
and through the mercy that makes all things new. Complete.

Perfect. My identity is in Him. Only *He* has the right to name me. As a matter of fact, only *He* has the right to name *you*.

My heart beat a little faster as I wrote down the names He had given me. Later, I followed each with a Scripture reference, but at the time, just seeing the list of names overwhelmed me. I pictured each word as a name tag.

Hello, My Name Is _____
Brave
Understood
Loved
Precious
Found
Worthy
Successful
Forgiven
Whole
Beautiful
Able
Wise
Genuine
Enough
A daughter

Setting the notebook aside, I laced up my tennis shoes and made my way to the back woods, where Flash liked to pass the afternoons in the shade of the tall oaks. At the sound of my call, his hooves rustled toward me through the underbrush.

"Flash! Hey, buddy." He came to a standstill in front of me and lowered his head to sniff my shirt and rub his forehead on my stomach. What a difference from the scared donkey he'd been just weeks ago. Perhaps ownership had changed him as well. He seemed eager for a good, all-over scratching, and I couldn't resist giving him one as I continued to ponder.

If you've ever had a paradigm shift, can you relate to how it feels like giant boulders are moving from one side of your brain to another? I tilted my head to hasten the process, and I'm not sure it helped, but I still couldn't deny that something big had happened. Something solidified.

> I belong to God. I am His.
> My identity is in Him. He has given me a new name.
> I am not what I do.
> My value doesn't come from my successes or
>   my failures.
> What I do comes from who I am, not the other
>   way around.
> My value is inherent, not earned.

No, I didn't hear any peals of thunder or angel choirs singing, and no trumpets blared to announce a "Hear Ye, Hear Ye" truth to my hurting heart. There was just this funny-looking burro who had landed on our doorstep late one night. And there in the back woods, while scratching a donkey's ears, I learned an incredible thing: God can use anything, at any time, in any way, to speak to me.

Fortunately, He was far from finished.

> Remember your name.
> Know whose you are.

CHAPTER 3
The Arctic Blast

If you're a person who likes certainty, then come on down to Texas in July. You are certain to experience searing temperatures that top one hundred degrees each and every day. You can depend on wide blue skies, punctuated by puffy white clouds that offer only fleeting moments of shade before leaving you to bake once again under the blistering sun. Most assuredly, you'll run from air-conditioned buildings to air-conditioned cars to air-conditioned buildings, clutching a sweater for the chilly indoor climates while perspiring profusely in between entries. You'll suddenly understand Southerners' deep affection for sweet tea and lemonade and realize that cowboy hats aren't only an icon of the West, but a way of avoiding sunburned necks and faces.

Lauren and Robert had picked July for their wedding but also had the sense to get hitched inside a church with powerful air conditioners. The frosting on the cake held tight, which was more than I could say for my hair that drooped like melted ganache. But that's only a small footnote on a wondrous event; despite the heat, it was a picture-perfect wedding.

Texas summers seem to stretch endlessly, the hot wind blasting across the prairies and withering all but the hardiest of vegetation. Day after sweltering day, those of us who live here find ourselves yearning for that first cool breeze that tells us autumn is on its way with the northern jet stream.

Now autumn, as far as seasons go, is a real guessing game.

You never know if you're going to get gorgeous fall colors on the trees, or if the leaves will simply turn brown and fall off. I've been told it has something to do with the amount of rain during the year, but really, it's all conjecture. No one really knows. We're all happy to have survived the heat, so vibrant leaf color is merely a bonus, like having gravy on your chicken-fried steak. Don't even get me started on winter weather.

But since you brought it up, let's just say Texas winters are crazy. They bring huge fluctuations in weather patterns, resulting in the obvious: an extreme dependence on hair products. Every woman in Texas lives in a state of perpetual preparedness. Word to the wise: If you know what's good for you, *do not* get between me and my can of superhold hair spray. A day in January might be sunny and seventy-five degrees, and the next day will likely bring freezing temperatures and biting winds that can knock the breath right out of you . . . and reduce your carefully coifed "hair-do" to a limp "hair-was." In seconds. But hair problems notwithstanding, I secretly enjoy the schizophrenic winters because I like waking up to surprises. Especially ones that bring flip-flop–wearing sunshine and a chance to wear shorts in midwinter.

With such extremes, it was necessary to have a suitable shelter for Flash, and our three-sided barn made a perfect home. He could go in and out as he pleased, finding welcome shade for loafing on a summer day and protection from the unpredictable wind, rain, and sleet during other times of the year.

"Flash still prefers the woods," Tom observed. "I think he likes to keep his options open." Nonetheless, under Flash's watchful eyes, Tom installed a hayrack and water bucket in the barn, shored up the partition, and hung lighting so we could see at night. These improvements received Flash's stamp of approval, with the hayrack being his most cherished feature of all. You would have thought his hay was being served up on fine china, as he eagerly pulled it from the sturdy metal structure, one mouthful at a time. It was fine dining, donkey style. When not eating or combing the floor for any dropped bits of hay, Flash's favorite place to station himself was half in and half out of the stall opening. Back end protected, front end out where he could see what was going on. With soft wood shavings on the dirt floor, Flash had a comfy spot for dozing. Pretty nice digs for a once-homeless fellow, and it felt good to see him enjoy the space.

As the seasons changed, Flash himself seemed to transform with them. His sleek, summery hair was again replaced by a thick, furry coat that made him appear fuzzy and chunky—a look that was endearing on him. The hair on his forehead and down his nose curled in all directions, giving him a kind of plump, teddy bear charm, and the creamy white hair on his chest and belly felt as soft as velvet and twice as deep. Every time I saw him, I just wanted to squeeze him, so I usually did.

Flash was getting accustomed to my bursts of affection, and though he pretended to simply tolerate them, I noticed he'd started to come running when I called. However, as soon as he got near me, he'd pull up and act like he just "happened" to be passing by. "Oh, you want to hug me? Well, if you must, I guess it's okay," Flash's demeanor intimated, barely hiding his delight. Perhaps in his previous life he'd been disappointed so often that he didn't want to appear too eager.

Nonchalance, as I'd found in my own experience, is an effective defense mechanism. Seeing it linger in him touched me, and I squeezed him a little more tightly because of it. And since winter had arrived, I threw in an extra handful of hay, which, in contrast, he received with joyous snorts and nickers. Not the slightest bit of indifference to be found.

February arrived, bringing a week of delightfully warm weather. Out came the shorts and sandals. Of course, it was immediately followed by a record-breaking cold front dubbed "The Arctic Blast" by local media. It hurled in from the north with freezing rain that brought our busy lives to a standstill. It probably goes without saying that Texans don't function well in ice, but I thought I'd go ahead and mention it. The pelting ice storm started during the night and continued throughout the following day, and all roads were shut down. Bridges and overpasses became slippery death traps. School attendance was unthinkable. We sat glued to our television set like weather zombies. *A jackknifed 18-wheeler on I-35? We must watch this.*

As the trees and native grasses became encrusted with layer upon layer of ice, they glittered eerily like a scene recreated from a Narnian winter. The temperatures dropped further, and the sleet kept coming as the deciduous trees began to bow under the weight. The branches of the cedars around the house were also bending beneath the load of ice; by nightfall they nearly touched the ground.

Inside, I turned on all the lamps and lit scented candles to celebrate being cozy and safe and warm on such an unforgiving night. The kids were already in their pajamas and sat on a rug by the fireplace with Beau, who was only too happy to join them as they started a movie. Canceled school meant a late-night treat for everyone, including the dog. Tom, a nature enthusiast, wasn't content to nestle in the comfort of our living room. I watched him don his jacket and hat.

"Where do you think you're going, honey?" I asked as he pulled on thick gloves. I had already guessed what his response would be.

"I've got to see how bad it is out there."

Tom always secretly hopes for a Texas blizzard—not surprising for someone who grew up in Minnesota and harbors an intense fascination with wintry blasts. *Mercy, he'd love a good snowstorm.* But short of a blizzard—the weather event of his dreams—ice is clearly the next best thing to snow. He'd never forgive himself if he missed it. Moments after closing the door behind him, he poked his nose back inside.

"Come out here with me," he called. I had seen enough with one glimpse—it looked awfully cold and miserable out there.

I shook my head and sank a little deeper into my afghan on the couch. *No. I'm good. Thank you, though.* Seriously, I felt quite comfortable inside where it was nice and warm. My fuzzy socks were delightful.

"Please come. I want you to experience this!" he insisted, his blue eyes dancing.

Sighing, I set my book facedown on the cushion, got up, and dutifully put on a heavy coat and shoes. Grayson and Meghan looked on in amusement. They were accustomed to their father's weather obsession and had already set out seldom-used plastic saucers for hill sliding with him in the morning. I followed him out into the icy evening, and he put his arm around me as we stepped across the crunchy grass.

"Rach, you've *got* to see this!" Tom said. He acts just like a kid during these climatic occurrences. I had to smile. Despite myself, I always get drawn into his excitement for the simple things.

He whipped out his high-powered flashlight and aimed the

beam into the trees. They shimmered in the light, their glittery layers of ice flashing and sparkling. The baubles of ice that clung to the cedars sounded like a thousand beaded dresses swaying in the cold night breeze.

He was right. It was worth coming outside. *And to think it didn't cost a penny.*

"Now," Tom said, "behold!" In a grand gesture, he moved the beam out into the pasture, where the winter grasses stood frozen in their white couture. Each blade, each plant, each stick was a picture of magical perfection, as if coated with glimmering fairy dust against the black sky.

"Ohhh," I breathed. It looked simply amazing. We stood awestruck by the beauty and savored it in the darkness that surrounded us. Tom slowly directed the shaft of light across the small field and toward the barn. The light tipped the grass and shrubs as it moved along, igniting icy sparkles in its path.

Suddenly a dark, shaggy lump appeared in the spotlight. Tom backed up and shone his flashlight across the gray mass again. *What in tarnation?*

Flash! Huddled just outside the barn in the freezing rain, the donkey raised his heavy head and peered back at us questioningly. "Huh?" he seemed to say. He started toward us, and as he neared, we could see that he, too, was covered in thick ice. Only on Flash, the ice coat wasn't nearly as glamorous as the one worn by the cedars. Crusty, frozen dirt balls stuck to his long winter hair, and a mass of muddy icicles hung from his mane. He was a cold, filthy mess.

"Flash, what are you doing?" I scolded him. "Why on earth are you standing outside the barn when you should be inside where it's nice and dry?" I'd checked on him earlier in the day and made sure he knew he had plenty of hay in the open stall. I never imagined he'd choose to brave the elements instead.

Flash pulled up close to the gate and gave me a pathetic look that said, "Please let me come into your cozy house to get warm."

Well, there wasn't a chance in the world that *that* was going to happen, but before I could open my mouth to set him straight, Tom turned to me and said, "Why don't you head back inside? I'm going to give the poor guy some oats."

"He'll just think you're rewarding him for his ignorance," I called after him, but to no avail. My man was already off to have mercy on the frosty beast who couldn't seem to figure out how to escape the sleet. I shook my head. *Aww, Flash! You're awfully cute, but where's your common sense tonight?*

Tom gave a whistle, which had become his signature call, and Flash followed across the frozen pasture to the barn. Once inside the shelter of the stall, Tom gave him a handful of oats and then made a hasty trip to the house for some supplies: towels, blankets . . . and a hair dryer. Back he went to the barn, and Flash shivered uncontrollably while Tom pulled the ice clods off him and blotted his matted hair with my good bath towels. Flash was soaked all the way to the skin—and dangerously cold. With one hand around his thick neck to reassure him, Tom turned on the noisy hair dryer. Flash startled and tried to break free.

"It's okay, Flash. We've got to get you dry." Tom began to work him over, inch by inch.

Once he got used to the whirring sound, the donkey relaxed and let the warm air blow over him. Gently separating Flash's hair, Tom massaged the animal's body with his fingers. Flash clearly loved the attention, cooperating fully by turning this way and that so that no part of him was missed. He chewed slowly on the hay, pausing whenever Tom hit a particularly pleasant spot. *Just above the tail? Oh yes, please.*

By the time Tom finished the lengthy salon treatment, Flash's hair felt soft and fluffy as it curled up along his back in shiny ringlets. Tom decided he was finally dry enough to drape with a heavy blanket (also one of my good ones) and leave for the night.

"Feel better now, buddy?"

Flash gave a deep sigh and pressed Tom's jacket sleeve with his white muzzle. With eyes closed and hindfoot resting, he was the picture of sleepy gratitude.

After one last noggin scratch, Tom returned to the house and shed his dirty jacket and hat. Cupping his hands under the hot water, he started to wash up as he gave me the report on our now-fluffed-and-warmed donkey.

"I can't figure out why he didn't get out of the sleet this afternoon," Tom said. "He could have been warm and dry this whole time, but it was like he didn't know how to take shelter in the barn when it was right in front of him."

I took the kettle off the stove to fill a mug with hot cocoa. "What could possibly have been going through his mind? I thought his sense of self-preservation would keep him inside." It was a mystery. "Anyway, thank you for getting him fixed up."

"Glad to do it." Tom took the mug from my hands and sat down in his recliner. I was grateful he had taken it upon himself to make sure Flash was safe. It was beyond the kind of cold I wanted to face that night. *Brrrr.* I went back to my book, but a word Tom had said niggled at me. I thought for a moment. What was it?

Shelter.

That was it.

It was the thing Flash had needed the most, and it had been available to him from the moment the storm hit. Just a few small steps would have taken him right inside, and he'd have been spared the dangerous misery he experienced as the ice and temperatures fell that day. I pictured him as he stood there, becoming coated with sleet, and yet unable, or unwilling, to seek shelter. I felt both sorry for him and puzzled by his behavior. I couldn't understand it.

Setting the book down once again, I suddenly had a vision of my own self—in the darkest moments of my life—standing outside, cold and alone, just as Flash had been. Oh sure, there had been many times I'd needed help and had been comforted by the shelter of God's presence. But there had also been just as many times that I'd stood shivering in lonely misery. Could it be possible that in my own moments of deepest need I had been just that close to comfort and not realized it?

Refuge—true refuge in the face of life's struggles—can be found only in Him. *I know that.* So why was it that when times got tough for us, the first thing I wanted to do was go shopping for a new purse? And eat something completely decadent, like a molten death-by-chocolate dessert topped with gooey ice cream? It's like I wanted to find comfort in the mall. Or more specifically, the food court of the mall. Or both.

Sometimes my refuge du jour was losing myself online in Facebook and Twitter. Doing Google searches for red-carpet hairstyles or shopping on Amazon. I never got into alcohol, but I hear it does a bang-up job of numbing pain. I've got plenty of little "coping techniques" for stress and storms, but in reality all of them are just substitutes for true comfort. Temporary relief for my deeper problems. They are counterfeits that seem like the real thing, but in the end, don't work.

I was learning the hard way that counterfeits in general can get you into trouble. I'm reminded of the time not long ago when an invitation to a wedding taught me this valuable lesson. I made a last-minute stop at the store for a gift and something to wear because, as per usual, I had nothing suitable on hand. Now running late, I dashed home and threw on my new outfit, then realized the clothes I'd so hurriedly bought would show the dreaded panty lines. *Yikes.* I rummaged like a madwoman through my drawers and baskets for my SPANX, the miracle outfit fixer, but could not come up with it anywhere.

Not to worry. In the deep recesses of my memory, a fashion tip I'd once heard surfaced: If you're in a pinch for a bottom-smoother, simply cut the legs off of a pair of panty hose and slide the top part on for a perfect substitute.

Eureka!

I grabbed some scissors, sliced the legs away from an old pair, and put them on. Fabulous idea—I was set. And so proud of my innovation. But perhaps I should point out that the title of this little illustration should be "Things That Seemed like Great Ideas at the Time But Did Not Live Up to Expectations."

The modified panty hose indeed work great in theory . . . for about the first hour. But after some time elapses, the problems set in.

I had made it all the way through the ceremony and into the reception when I realized that my science wasn't as sound as I'd assumed. As I stood up to get more cheese from the appetizer table, the cutoff edges of my faux SPANX rolled up to my derriere like Cuban cigars, creating a visual disaster zone. *Way too much cheese, my friends.*

Mortified, I stiffly made my way to the ladies' room for an adjustment and decided to stand for the rest of the reception. There would be no dancing that day.

I learned, via personal humiliation, that there is no substitute for the Real Thing.

Oh, the Bible has so much to say about the Real Thing—the true kind of refuge that is found in its pages. It's one of those subjects that makes my ears perk up when I hear it, maybe because I need it so often. Refuge—something that brings comfort to the soul—is one of our deepest needs as human beings. We long for it. And when you consider why we do the things we do, the need for refuge fuels most of the activity in the world.

Webster's dictionary defines *refuge* this way: "protection or shelter, as from danger or hardship; a source of help, relief, or comfort in times of trouble."

Refuge, in a practical sense, is

Safety: protection from outside forces, the "storms of life"

Security: freedom from fear, which allows you to flourish

Significance: being confident in your place in the world; your contribution

Provision: having your physical, emotional, and spiritual needs met

Belonging: knowing you are part of something bigger than yourself

I thought of the times I'd experienced a vague sense of unease and unsettledness that was hard to put a finger on. And when weariness, like the kind I had when Flash showed up on our doorstep, had settled deeply in my bones. Something seemed to be missing, *but what?* I was going through the motions of parenting and working and serving, but I felt like there was a hole in the middle of it all. Perhaps it was the "significance" factor or the aspect of "belonging" that I wasn't experiencing, and inside I simply longed for some kind of refuge.

And then there were other times in which the circumstances of life were too painful to bear, when the vague unease became absolute desperation for comfort.

∧ ∧

I was about to turn forty, and two faint pink lines on a stick from a test kit told me I was pregnant—ten years after our youngest child had been born, fifteen and seventeen years after our daughters. Once the surprise (and let's be honest, *panic*) wore off, excitement set in. This was the child we had desired for so long, had hoped for, and had given up on ever having.

It thrilled me that I would get to experience mommyhood all over again! I loved those years with little ones and could not believe we were going to be blessed with a fourth baby. And both my sister and sister-in-law were expecting babies within days of my due date! What were the chances of that happening? We surprised my mother with back-to-back Mother's Day phone calls telling her our news. The whole family was elated.

And then our excitement was cut short.

"I'm so sorry," the doctor said, tears filling her eyes in sympathy as she moved the ultrasound wand over my abdomen. My heart pounded out of my chest as I clutched Tom's hand in the small examination room. We scanned the dark screen, desperate to see any sign of movement, but there was nothing. Just a tiny, lifeless form that had been our baby.

Just a few weeks before, in an effort to break up the monotony of a long, hot summer day, I was making a spontaneous run to the video store with Grayson when our vehicle was hit head-on by a distracted driver on a country road. We felt lucky to walk away from the wreck unscratched, and I immediately went to the doctor to make sure the baby's heartbeat was still there. What a relief to hear it! But it didn't last.

"Abruption of the placenta," they called it—the result of trauma. In sudden shock and grief, the floor fell away from my feet, the room spinning around us.

They give you twenty-four hours to absorb the news before inducing labor. They tell you to go home and rest, that it will all soon be over. They tell you it is "nature's way" and that you'll be able to have other babies, don't worry. What they don't tell you is how hard you'll cry, or how alone you'll feel, or that your heart will break in a million pieces while you wait. They don't tell you that labor, when you know at the end of it you'll have no baby to bring home, is horrific. They don't tell you that when your milk comes in and there is no baby to nurse, you'll sit in the shower and sob until you can't sob anymore. They don't tell you any of that.

But then, nothing can prepare you for this kind of disappointment, this much heartache.

Tom and I got to see our little boy in the delivery room. We named him Collin, and he was beautiful. So utterly perfect. There was a small funeral and a tiny casket under an awning in the rain . . . and so many questions. I wished God had left us well enough alone. We'd been content with three wonderful, healthy children—why on earth had He snatched Collin away so cruelly, only pretending to give us another precious gift?

For months I could not stop the tears that would come, unbidden, as I washed dishes or folded clothes, or drove along on the country road where the cars had collided and my happy little world had ended. I couldn't bear the holidays; the thought of seeing my sister and sister-in-law's pregnant bellies was too much, so we stayed away. I felt a constant lump in my throat, and I squeezed my eyes shut so I wouldn't think of the precious life—the little fingers and toes and belly button—that we would never know.

I needed refuge. Comfort for the anguish that engulfed me.

I clung to Psalm 34:18—"The LORD is close to the broken-hearted; he rescues those whose spirits are crushed"—as well as Psalm 145:14—"The LORD upholds all who fall and lifts up all who are bowed down" (NIV). *Jesus, please. Please be close to me.* Most days I could not sense Him anywhere. But there was *something* that had occurred during the long night before I was scheduled for labor that gave me the tiniest glimmer of hope, a trace of refuge that somehow carried me. It was unexplainable.

It happened when the old clock radio next to my bed clicked on at a time no one had set it for. As I struggled to figure out why the radio was on at this strange hour, a song by Fernando Ortega began to play. "Jesus, King of Angels" poured over me like warm honey. That's the only way I can describe it. I weighed a thousand pounds and could not move as the words gently dripped down into my soul and pooled there.

The lyrics reminded me that the infinite God of the universe is mindful of each sparrow that falls. *My baby. Oh, my little one.*

He was mindful of all the anxious thoughts that filled me, and He would be with me and keep me in His peace. The final notes of the guitar faded.

Tears, and more tears. My pillow was soaked with them. I lay in the predawn gray hours and ached for the baby I was about to deliver, the one I would never get to know. I dreaded the hours, days, and weeks that were to come. And yet my heart replayed the song hundreds of times as the dark days passed, a reminder that His presence was with me, even when I could not feel Him or understand the whys.

There was a hint of a promise that one day I would again rise to speak the goodness of His name, and there was comfort, even in my ashes. The recurring melody pulled me those last few feet into the shelter that was just beyond me. I was warm and safe and dry, even in the midst of hurting.

Just like Flash on that cold, icy night.

∧ ∧

I went to the window, which was now glazed with a fine sheet of ice. Through it, I could see the amber glow of the stall lights shining through the darkness and spilling onto the frozen ground beyond. And I knew in my heart that I was being pulled close once again.

Psalm 91:1-2 says,

Those who live in the shelter of the Most High
    will find rest in the shadow of the Almighty.
This I declare about the LORD:
He alone is my refuge, my place of safety;
    he is my God, and I trust him.

I tucked in tightly under His shadow. Chose to trust in His care. Leaned into His comfort.

Shelter.

Sanctuary.

Refuge.

God's presence is always with us, even when we can't feel or see Him. Even when we can't understand our circumstances. And though we might try a million other ways to fill our voids and find shelter from our storms, there is no substitute for the real thing. Only God can be our true source of refuge.

How many times do we stand outside in the cold when shelter is so close at hand? Sometimes all it takes is a few more steps—and then we are in His arms, encircled in His care and carried by His comfort.

He has all the fresh towels and blankets we need.

Know where to find refuge.
True sanctuary is found in God alone.

CHAPTER 4

Flash Runs with Horses

It was early morning when Bridgette called. After the formal chitchat about how-are-the-kids-and-how-is-*Hay*-soos (eye roll), she got to her point.

"I've got a wonderful opportunity for your talents," she said. "Please pardon my huffing and puffing. I'm trying to get my power walk in while I talk."

"No problem," I replied. I was still in my bathrobe, but that wouldn't keep me from discussing business. I poured a second cup of coffee and grabbed a chocolate chip cookie, the breakfast of champions.

It seemed that she and Steve had been hired to design and oversee the finish-out of a corporate building in Fort Worth, a project that would include a restaurant and call center.

"This would be *per*-fect for you and Tom," Bridgette remarked with enthusiasm. "It's just one big, blank canvas, and your creativity will make it come to life. It needs custom finishes, artwork, signage, and furniture. And, by the way, we'd like to hire you to head up the FF&E."

Bridgette continued on, discussing issues and describing her vision for the space, her effusive voice filling my ear. But I wasn't following it. I was still stuck on "FF&E." *FF&E?* Never heard of it. Were they actual letters, or a word spelled *effeffeny?* I didn't want to appear foolish, so I played along while she threw out other trade acronyms she obviously assumed I knew. I caught what I could and furiously scribbled notes so I could look things up later.

"Wow, sounds like a great project," I said confidently. "We'd love to be part of it!" Bridgette's energy and excitement were contagious, and somehow even her use of inside industry terms made me feel ready to take on the world. Our mural business was still bumping along, and this was exactly the break we'd been waiting for. We set a time to meet at the building site and then hung up.

My heart sank. The reality of having to present the ideas in person to the client suddenly hit me. *What was I thinking?* This job was way beyond the scope of anything we'd ever done, and I didn't understand even half of what Bridgette was talking about. Not only was this project going forward in a language I didn't understand . . . I also didn't have the wardrobe for it. Years of painting baby nurseries and cramped bathrooms had hardly prepared me for *effeffeny*, or whatever it was. It sounded so corporate and professional. This would not end well, I just knew it. My stomach turned at the thought.

Meanwhile, Tom was calling our place "some kind of circus," and he wasn't too far off in his assessment. It seemed every animal in the county made its way onto our property at one time or another: raccoons who regularly dined on Beau's dog food, opossums who loved picking apart our trash, mice running amok, coyotes, bobcats, snakes, stray dogs and cows . . . all looking for mischief, and they all seemed to find us.

In fact, shortly before Flash had arrived on the scene, we were awakened from sleep by four loose horses traipsing through our yard at midnight, followed by people in pickup trucks who were trying to round them up. Maybe it was the whoops, hollers, and blaring music that spooked the renegades, or perhaps it was the spinning tires, or the sound of beer bottles being thrown, or the crazy gunfire aimed skyward that made the horses run wildly in circles. Hard to tell. All we knew was that later, when a stray donkey showed up, it seemed like just another act in an animal circus gone awry.

By the time spring rolled around, Flash had become friends with the rather large and cumbersome cattle in the next pasture. As we educated ourselves about donkeys, we learned they are social creatures who are best kept with other donkeys. Unfortunately, that was not anywhere in our budget. Flash would have to fly solo for a while.

In the absence of another donkey, they might make do with a cow, horse, sheep, or goat. Anything but a dog, at least in Flash's case. Dogs (and coyotes) are donkeys' natural enemies, which explained a whole lot about Flash and Beau's chilly relationship. Still in a barking/kicking standoff with one another, each day found Flash at the back fence, preferring to fraternize with the fat bovines on the other side than with a slobbery, exuberant Lab. While the cows seemed mostly indifferent—lying down or standing with their heads through the fence for the "better" grass on our side—Flash hung out near them like a comfortable old companion.

The days were warming, and there was a slow, easy pace to life in the pasture. I wished I could say the same for life on the "people" side of the fence. The stream of marauding animals only complicated the juggling act of work and family. There was nothing like picking up the contents of an overturned garbage can after a gang of raccoons had picked through it, while still trying to make it to the day's job site on time. Country life, while much prettier than suburban life, takes a whole lot more work to maintain.

Finally, a weekend arrived that wasn't filled with hockey games and trips to Home Depot for project supplies. We could catch up on some of our own honey-dos for a change. I stood at the kitchen sink and plunged my hands into the sudsy water to tackle the pile of dishes from the night before.

Washing dishes didn't seem quite so bad when I had time to look out the window and watch Grayson untangle his fishing pole and sort the tackle box in the front yard. Beau lay beside him and yawned, clearly relaxed by the sound of spinners, jigs, and spooners being organized in the hard plastic container. Grayson closed the lid, and the large dog snapped to attention, instantly ready for a walk to the pond with his boy.

Pole over shoulder, tackle box in hand, dog at side. *Thank You, God, for this.*

I reached for a plate and dunked it into the water, still gazing through the window, past the yard to the wildflowers beyond. Suddenly, the moment was interrupted by three gorgeous horses who emerged from the woods and trotted into the front field. It was as if they materialized right before my eyes, *Star Trek* style.

Once in the clearing, they lowered their heads to graze, tails swishing and manes tossing. Young males, they exemplified equine perfection: a black horse with a white blaze down its nose; a chestnut with white socks and a long, dark mane and tail; and a paint with brown and white markings. My dish scrubbing immediately ceased as I leaned forward to take in the stunning beauty of these unexpected animals.

As a child, I'd been so horse-crazy that I drove my parents

nuts. Daily, I scoured the local newspaper in search of the perfect horse to put in our backyard. I was sure I'd find one that looked like Little Joe's on *Bonanza*, a beautiful paint that would be mine, all mine. I had it all planned out: We would spend lazy afternoons together—me braiding his tail and brushing him until he gleamed, and him carrying me over the countryside in full gallop. I would be beautiful and courageous atop my steed named Apache (Patch for short).

Unfortunately, as a preacher's family, we lived in town, and later we moved to Mexico City as missionaries—so neither location was suitable for keeping equines. My fantasy of having a horse had faded into quiet wistfulness as I grew up, but seeing these animals suddenly appear reminded me of my latent desire. *Too bad all we have is a dusty donkey.*

"Come take a look at this!" I called to Tom and Meghan, flinging suds as I motioned with wet hands. They hurried to the window for a peek at our latest four-legged guests.

"Those are Russell's horses." Tom identified them at first glance with a low, appreciative whistle. "Aren't they something!" He paused for a moment in admiration. "I've got his work number. I'll give him a call to let him know they're here. But first I'll get them locked up in our pasture for safekeeping."

Infinitely easier than catching one smallish donkey, Tom handily coaxed the three horses into following his oat-filled bucket. Piece of cake. Meghan opened the gate as they arrived and quickly shut it behind them with a clang of the chain on the metal crossbar. Tom and Meghan returned to the house so Tom could notify the owner.

"Russell can't get here with his trailer until after work," Tom said, holding a business card with the number scrawled on it.

He set his cell phone down and continued. "Looks like Flash will get to have company for the rest of the afternoon."

"This could be interesting! I wonder how he'll feel about sharing his space with these guys," I responded. I slipped into flip-flops and headed to the gate to see what would happen.

And what a sight to behold.

The afternoon sun cast a golden glow over the pasture and created a storybook scene in which the stallions took center stage. Prancing and playing, they seemed to dance effortlessly across the field. It was a horse ballet!

The sun glistened off their rippling muscles as they tossed their heads and galloped through the tall grass. Their shapely legs carried them around and around, while their manes and tails flowed out behind them in raw beauty. The strength and perfection of these creatures was a joy to watch. We rested our chests against the gate, elbows out and a foot on the lowest rung, and enjoyed the show.

Just then, a movement from the corner of the pasture caught our attention.

Flash.

Arrested from the spot near his beloved cows by this sudden intrusion of the equines, he shook his long ears as if trying to wake himself up. Bending around like a contortionist to scratch his rear end with his teeth, he brought a back foot up and set it down with a thud. We watched him flex his lips as the new company's arrival began to register in his brain. He blinked his black lashes until finally alert, then did a double take. Flash looked at the horses, and then back to the cows.

Horses, cows. Horses. Cows.

Hmmm.

Yep, horses. Definitely horses.

And without a backward glance, he ditched the cows for the newcomers.

Just like that, the cows were dead to him. He trotted over to meet his new posse.

Flash's sparse mane bristled back and forth as his choppy gait carried him to the trio. He pulled up next to the shiny black leader and raised his giant head in greeting. The horse turned his graceful neck to see the short donkey arrive and gave a snort. Ha! As if motioning to his friends, he nodded toward the opposite end of the pasture, and the three were off in a cloud of dust and hooves—only this time they were followed by Flash, who looked hopelessly outgunned and outclassed.

Next to the cows, Flash had seemed like a regal ruler of the landscape. His intelligent eyes and quick wit endeared him to the mindless, cud-chewing bovines who kept him company each afternoon. But now, with the arrival of the three ballerinos, Flash suddenly had some shortcomings, starting with his stature. Such stubby legs! And his head's proportion was conspicuously out of whack. My word, so *huge*! And the ears—oh, the ears.

But Flash did not care. He shifted into high gear and headed after the group, now circling at the far end of the pasture. Bucking and braying as he went, he joined up and fell into step with their show. They paused at his arrival, deciding whether or not to let this newcomer enter. *Please?* Flash seemed to say with his ears, all forward and hopeful. Someone whinnied in reply. One of them broke rank and allowed Flash in.

And in that instant, he was one of them.

The horses pranced.

Flash pranced.

The horses reared.

Flash reared.

The horses tossed their manes.

Flash tossed—well, *tried* to toss—his mane.

The horses glistened.

Okay. Flash didn't glisten. In fact, he magnetically *collected* all the kicked-up dust into his fuzzy gray coat.

But no matter. Flash was having the time of his life. He wheeled and turned and danced and cavorted. He chased and nuzzled and pawed and reared. He was ridiculous in his earnestness, but he was part of the horse ballet—and his little heart beat faster with each plié and spin.

Flash had burst into life, and every equine cell in his body was ablaze. *The soul of a thoroughbred in the body of a shaggy donkey.* What a picture; what a day. This was living, and I'd never seen him look so endearing. The setting sun outlined his form in golden fringe as his pace slowed to a graceful *adagio* around the three horses. Circling, spinning, moving. The cows looked on in disbelief. What had happened to their quiet, unassuming friend? They hardly recognized him with his new air of confidence and all.

Evening fell like a gossamer curtain over the field, and Russell arrived with his dual truck and horse trailer to load up the gorgeous guests and take them home. With a slam of the trailer door and a roar of diesel, they were gone, and Flash stood at the gate with ears pricked and trembling. His nostrils flared, and his sides heaved as he stifled his bellows. He watched the trailer turn the corner and disappear down the driveway. Something had happened to him that day, and even *he* knew it.

He was changed.

He was bigger, stronger, and more powerful than before.

He showed confidence.

He held his head higher.

He carried himself boldly.

He'd become fearless.

And all because he'd run with horses.

It was as though he had suddenly realized his own greatness. As if someone had told him that donkeys and horses were nearly identical in genetic makeup. That they shared the same chromosomes—sixty-two of them, in fact. The *only* difference between donkeys and horses is an *extra* set of two chromosomes that horses carry. An extra set that Flash didn't need in the least.

I thought about Flash and his visitors long afterward.

Maybe he'd been told all his life that he'd never amount to anything because he lacked the two units that would make him great. Maybe he spent all his time thinking about how his mane didn't blow in the wind and how his gait was bumpy and how silly he'd look if he tried running. Maybe he'd always compared himself with horses and come up short every time. Maybe nobody ever told him that he has 97 percent of the same chromosomes as those horses . . . or that the horses needed two *less* to be just like *him*.

Maybe nobody ever told him that *he has all the chromosomes he needs* to be a perfect donkey.

I wondered if, until now, Flash had been focused on the two he lacked, rather than on the sixty-two he had. I wondered if he'd told himself, as I had: *If only I'd finished my college degree.*

I wondered if he'd said: I'm not talented enough to run with the big boys. My ears are too big, my head too heavy, my legs too short, my bray too loud.

I wasn't born into money. Or looks. Or special intelligence.

I'm not graceful. I can't prance. I don't glisten.

I don't have business training. I'm too old. I drive an ancient Ford Explorer. I never took art lessons.

Looking at his lack had kept Flash with the cows—those lackluster, mediocre characters who sat and wished for better grass and more gumption.

Once again I found myself mirrored in this winsome donkey of mine. But this time, I saw what a change of perspective could do. Perhaps I needed to start focusing on my sixty-two, rather than the two. *Aw, Flash. You're a genius.*

∧ ∧

Of course, it's one thing to think something and quite another thing to actually do it. The project with Bridgette was officially underway, and it immediately tested my fledgling sense of empowerment.

"Be there at 1:00," Bridgette told me as we wrapped up another phone call about the interior design of the space. "We'll be in the conference room, and I've given you thirty minutes on the agenda to make a presentation to the board and the contractors."

Oh dear. That would have been a good moment to tell Bridgette that I have a debilitating fear of speaking in conference rooms to boards and contractors. Also to groups of two or more. It's this thing where my throat closes up and my mouth gets all dry and my vision goes blurry, just before I black out. I briefly imagined what it would be like to hit my head on the table as I was going down and then be laid up in a hospital with a skull injury for several weeks and only be able to eat Jell-O for every meal. The silver lining in that whole scenario was that I wouldn't have to make my presentation, and also I might possibly lose five pounds and not have to wear faux SPANX to weddings.

I wished I'd said all that, right then and there. But Bridgette was so persuasive and charming that for a moment I felt all confident, and I let myself get swept up in her energy. I danced, just a little bit, and it felt good. But maybe I should call her back and tell her I'd made a huge mistake and would not be able to make it to the meeting on account of my illness, or perhaps a broken leg. I could probably arrange an accident, or at least make a fake cast. I'm good at crafts. Anything to get out of this whole looming *effeffeny* catastrophe.

No. I had to go through with this. And it was then that I decided, shakily, to run with horses. Enough with the cows. I wanted to try glistening for once.

But it would take some work.

I found a drafting table on a curbside for twenty-five dollars, and Tom cleared a spot for it in the loft that overlooks the back room. We moved an old computer, brought in some lamps, and put a chair in place. I bought a portable filing box and started making good use of Internet searches, starting with "FF&E": Furniture, Fixtures, and Equipment.

Aha! *So that's what it means! I'm in charge of procuring furniture, fixtures, and equipment!* I spent an inordinate amount of time searching "How to Give a Winning Presentation" and "Fear of Public Speaking." I made a trip to the department store for some appropriate business attire (30 percent off) and picked up a briefcase at the thrift shop. I asked for Photoshop help from our kids. I became familiar with architectural drawings. Hair highlights would have to wait—rats!

But I was ready. And I got down to business. Tom and I both dug in and came up with ideas that stretched us, made us create new kinds of art, and caused us to see just how much we could do once we stopped focusing on why we couldn't do it.

And even though you could say we'd already taken our share of chances along the way (i.e., ditching regular jobs for a dreamy artistic one), we'd also let ourselves get comfortable in the types of projects we went for. The kinds of clients we thought we were good enough for. The jobs that didn't require making presentations and proposals on design boards in conference rooms to important people. We'd gotten passive in our approach and forgotten the power of putting ourselves out there on a bigger stage. We played small. Safe.

We'd counted the two chromosomes we lacked as more important than the sixty-two we had, and it had kept us in a place of mediocrity.

Flash had us beat by a mile.

You see, when someone opens a gate and gives you a shot at running with horses, the choice is yours. You can stay where you're at—comfortable, unchallenged, and wishing your life away—or you can step forward and decide that this is your moment. You can dance on your stubby little legs and collect everyone else's dust and maybe look foolish doing it. But you're *doing* it! That's the point. You find your thoroughbred heart in there somewhere, and you take the chance. You choose it. And you run with it.

"As [a man] thinks in his heart, so is he," says Proverbs 23:7

(NKJV). I wonder how many limits you've put on yourself by simply *thinking* incorrectly. By focusing on past failures, all the gifts and talents you think you don't have, and the abilities you believe everyone else has, you keep yourself in a position of *not being ready* when opportunity comes knocking. You choose cows over horses because cows are safe and accepting and think you're really awesome. It's so sweet. But they keep you by the fence, watching life from the sidelines. Chewing cud, offering opinions, and giving commentary on the ones who are out there getting something done.

You don't ever do anything that makes your heart race or your palms get sweaty, or that involves the risk of hitting your head on the way down. You stay busy and work hard and never have to consider that you're living in fear of being your best self.

Running with horses, on the other hand, means that you have to face your fears. The fear of looking foolish, the fear of failing big, the fear of speaking in public, of learning new software, of going beyond your comfort zone into the unknown. Maybe even the fear of your own success. It means that you count your sixty-two as *enough* for the task and then set your heart on excellence—being the best you can be.

Running with horses is risky. And I admired Flash for his plucky decision to up his game. It inspired me to risk blacking out during my presentation and to choose wide-legged trousers so no one would see my knees knock. Yes, my vision was a little blurry, and my mouth went dry, but somehow I survived my thirty minutes in that conference room. I didn't remember anything about it afterward, and that's beside the point. I may have even drooled a little bit. I can't think about that.

Here's what matters. I came to see how *one single fear*, the fear of public speaking, kept me from moving forward in my professional and personal life. How many ways can a person avoid leading a group discussion or teaching a class or making a presentation? I'd come up with a hundred different ones throughout my life in order to give my fear, *one set of two chromosomes*, a bigger place than the sixty-two. And it kept me from doing my best work, because no one ever gets asked to present mediocre ideas.

I decided to change all of that. I would no longer let fear be the reason to say no to something. If fear was the only thing that stood between me and a new opportunity, then the answer would have to be yes. (Jumping out of airplanes notwithstanding.) And I would use *excellence* as my weapon of choice to defeat the fear that wanted to paralyze me. Rather than focusing on the fear itself, I'd focus on doing—and being—excellent in my approach. I'd make the most of my sixty-two and run with those horses. Whatever happened next, well, I'd deal with it.

Excellence—going the extra mile, learning all you can, doing things better than you thought you could—brings confidence that trumps fear. It opens up doors and creates opportunities that mediocrity and fear never can. And it works on every level—not just in business.

What would happen if we stopped fearing having a dysfunctional family and simply focused on having an excellent family life? If we stopped wishing we'd had decent role models and just became ones ourselves?

Imagine if we quit worrying about losing weight and focused instead on being in excellent health. We'd choose foods and make lifestyle choices that would energize us so we could rock our worlds.

What if, rather than bemoaning a lack of deep friendships in our lives, we worked at being excellent friends to others?

Rather than letting ourselves be convinced that we aren't smart enough for that job promotion or that degree, what if we focused on gaining the skills and knowledge to make it happen?

Instead of sitting at the back of the room where we can't be noticed, what if we found seats at the front and raised our hands to ask questions?

Or rather than wishing we were born with artistic genes, what if we picked up a paintbrush or camera and found that creative skills can be learned? Maybe we'll never be Picassos or Ansel Adamses, but it doesn't matter. We can achieve far more by doing than by simply watching.

Doing makes you try harder, reach further, and achieve more than you thought you could. Action propels you toward excellence and makes the impossible—possible.

Yes, when you run with horses, you run the risk of stumbling and looking foolish. . . . But oh, what a way to go. There is greatness inside of you, looking for a chance to burst into life and kick up some dust. You will be stretched and challenged and pushed because the bar has been raised. You'll have to reach deep to find what's inside you.

But you are up to it. Remember your sixty-two.

The sixty-two that make you the perfect donkey.

Just like Flash. Just like me.

Run with horses.
The pursuit of excellence conquers fear.

CHAPTER 5

A Pasture Romance

lash's social life was looking up. Not long after his momentous dance with the elegant horses, some new people moved into the ranch behind us. A portion of their sprawling land abutted the north end of Flash's pasture on one side, while the cows' fence bordered the south end. This arrangement gave the ever-curious Flash a perfect vantage point to see what was going on around him.

One day, we noticed some horses grazing in the north pasture. Flash now had his pick of whom he'd like to spend his lazy afternoons with—the horses or the cows. I wasn't surprised at his decision; Flash's newfound confidence made him ally squarely with the horses.

"This will have to satisfy Flash's social needs for now," Tom said as he watched them touch noses over the fence. "I'm a little relieved, actually. All the benefits of having more animals without the work and expense."

Flash was happy as could be with this new arrangement. He lifted his pliable upper lip to show his teeth, rocking his head from side to side in greeting. Did it bother him that he had a leaf between his front teeth? Nope. Not in the least. He just smiled away, fully confident of the effect of his donkey charm on the mares next door, who seemed amused but thoroughly unimpressed.

"Honey, let me help you finish loading the truck," I offered, grabbing a plastic bin filled with paints and brushes. Tom was departing for a work marathon to complete the installation of the art for Bridgette's corporate project. It looked like it was going to take an all-nighter to meet the deadline. Bridgette and Steve had championed our skills and convinced the project managers that we could not only create and install custom artwork but also design signage and wayfinding for the spaces as well.

As we had suspected, the job was indeed beyond our previous experience, and it required some on-the-job training to pull it off. But the scope of the project made us find some talent we didn't know we'd had. We leaned on our daughter and new son-in-law to give us those crash courses in Photoshop and learned graphic design as we went along. The medium was new, but the principles and the skills we'd honed over years of creating mural art were the same. There was an excitement to the work—a sink-or-swim feeling that carried us through the weeks of design and installation. We were, indeed, running with horses.

That night, we had decided to divide and conquer the workload, so I stayed at our home office and poured myself an extra cup of coffee to work on some last-minute drawings that were needed. By 1:00 a.m., I was bleary but determined to finish.

Then, without warning, the bright red and blue lights of a squad car pierced the darkness outside the window. My heart stopped for a second as I assessed the situation. No cars ever drive up our remote driveway late at night, let alone a police vehicle! This could not be good. I peered through the glass as two sheriff's deputies hoisted themselves out of the front seat and came up the walk.

"Howdy, ma'am," one of the men said as I opened the door a crack. In my mind I could see the headline—"Woman Slain by Phony Sheriffs Overnight"—followed by a story with a stern warning to women to not open their doors for just anyone who flashes a badge.

As if on cue, the officers flashed their badges, and I felt certain they were probably murderers—but I went ahead and opened the door wider to get it over with. The two men were exactly what you might picture Texas county sheriff's deputies looking like: imposing and serious, with crew cuts, and with builds that hinted at both weightlifting and doughnuts. Their starched uniforms were pulled taut across their chests, and suddenly I felt more threatened by an impending button pop-off than the Colt .45s in their holsters. Plus, their car looked somewhat legit with the lights and all.

"Sorry to bother you, ma'am," the lead deputy said. "I'll cut right to the chase." He paused for a moment. "Uh, you own a donkey?"

Sir, you're pulling up at this hour, with lights flashing, to ask me if I own a donkey?

Just then, a pickup truck roared up the driveway and came to a stop behind the squad car. Two vehicles in one night? This was some kind of record. The truck door burst open, and out stumbled a man, a waft of beer and stale cigars hanging on him.

"Yes, yes, I do," I replied, narrowing my eyes and thinking what a good setup this was. The fake officers disarm me with their badges while the boss pulls up to finish the job. I was a goner, for sure. If only I'd had time to leave a note for the kids.

"Well, this gentleman here," said the deputy, motioning over his shoulder, "says you got a problem on your hands."

I looked questioningly over to the new guy, who stepped forward, apparently to tell me all about it. It was then that I wondered about a justice system in which some kind of "donkey problem" is deemed greater than the fact that this man may have driven under the influence to inform me in person. *What kind of society is this, anyway? And why aren't the officers arresting this man?*

"Yore donkey . . . ," he slurred, pointing his finger in my face. "Yore donkey got up into my corral and got at my mare. I'd been keepin' her away from my stallions, and then yore sorry little donkey broke in and got to her." He swayed toward me and continued. "Yeah, he got to her, all right. By the time I figured it out and found 'em, they was layin' down, smokin' a cigarette. The deed had been done."

I blinked at him in horror as he capped off his story. "Lady, yore gonna have a baby mule on yore hands, 'cause that's what you get when you cross a donkey with a horse. A baby mule!" He kicked at some gravel in disgust and let his words hang in the air.

There was an awkward pause as I struggled for an appropriate response. Something about Flash being an "immature" male and incapable of procreation. Something about how he was too young for this kind of monkey business. Wait. Had maturity happened while we'd been up to our necks in our new project, not paying attention to the passage of time and adolescence? *Uh-oh.*

The deputy cleared his throat and asked, "You gonna go get him tonight then?"

I turned to him and said, "Tonight? I can't drag him home in the middle of the night! Can't this wait until morning? The 'deed' has been done, so what's the hurry?" Also, I was in my slippers.

The deputy looked at the man. The horse owner shrugged,

the fight suddenly gone out of him. He got back in his truck, slumped behind the steering wheel, and said out the door, "Just get him tomorrow; it's already too late."

∧ ∧

Morning dawned, and Tom fell into bed, exhausted from the all-night art installation. I decided right then to deal with the donkey situation on my own, so I kept quiet about Flash's escapade, tucked Tom in, and tiptoed out. I would need tools, so I headed for the local feed store.

"Give me the largest halter you've got," I said to the lady at the register. I slapped my hand down on the counter and looked around the joint like I knew what I was doing.

"Sure. Whatcha got, a hefty Belgian?" she asked, snapping her gum and indicating his height with her hand over her head.

I sighed. "No. No, just a smallish donkey . . . with a gigantic head." I held my hand chest-high. "I've got to get him home from my neighbor's house, so I'll need some oats and a lead rope as well."

Just then, my cell phone rang. It was my friend Priscilla. She and I had met a few years earlier when she'd found my business card and hired me to paint her baby's nursery. We hit it off immediately and spent so much time talking with each other that the one-week job took about three weeks to complete. Our differences in age, vocation, ethnicity, and life season didn't matter one bit as we sat on that nursery room floor and dreamed up a beautiful space for the new baby.

Later, even though I had retreated into my work and family responsibilities, she kept after me. Gradually, through her determined effort to break through my wall of busyness, we became real friends, and over time I had come to count her as family. She now had two babies in tow, and I hoped to convince her that she and her husband needed to move to the country to raise their family. I thought a house on our quiet road would be a perfect place for them.

"What are you doing?" she asked. I started to give her the lowdown, but before I could finish, she said, "I'm on my way," and hung up. Priscilla was always up for an adventure, and what better way to initiate her into country life than to chase down a loose farm animal?

The August air was stifling by the time we donned tennis shoes and got ourselves organized. It was going to be a hot one. Accompanied by the deafening sound of cicadas overhead, Priscilla and I made our way to the pasture's back gate, which had been ripped from its hinges by my precious little donkey. *Mercy!*

We walked farther to find a broken fence post, wires dangling. A little farther, and another broken fence. *Dear me.* I dreaded to see what kind of state Flash would be in after all this. We finally found him holed up in the corral next to his ladylove, beat up from his night of charging through barbed wire fences and foisting his affection upon her.

Just one look at him told me he was not going to come easily. He had the same hardened donkey stare as the first night we'd found him—"Make me," it simply said.

So we haltered him up and started coaxing.

Flash would have none of it. And who could blame him? The leggy mare he'd fallen for was adorable. Chocolate brown in color with a black mane and tail, she was an exotic vixen, and he was a lovesick donkey-boy. He was hopelessly, madly, genuinely in love with her. She, on the other hand, was not so much in love with him but clearly in love with being adored. With her head tossing and hooves prancing, she accepted this lopsided relationship with her body language. That was all Flash needed to see; he was fully committed to making the tenuous bond work. Now, with head low and blubbering lips pulled back, he sullenly brayed his opposition to our mission to move him.

Flash refused to leave his girlfriend, whom we now called "Maria," after the female lead in *West Side Story*. At the prospect of being forced apart, she decided she'd make it work as well. Maria whinnied at him and paced back and forth in her corral as we inched him away from her. Hours of pushing, pulling, cajoling, entreating, and offering treats yielded only limited progress. We were still on the neighbor's property, just halfway to the back gate, and standing at an impasse in the blistering sun.

"We've tried everything," Priscilla said, wiping the perspiration from her forehead. "The only thing we haven't tried is dropping the rope to see if he'll come on his own." She reminded me that, under normal circumstances, Flash follows us around like a puppy dog. He can't stand to be left behind.

"True," I said, unconvinced but willing to try anything at this point. "We might as well give it a go. What do we have to lose?"

So we dropped the rope and turned to head back to our place. We took teeny little pretend steps, glancing over our shoulders to see what Flash would do.

"And we're walking away. We're walking, and we're leaving . . ." I narrated our movements for good measure, just in case Flash didn't notice that we were leaving him.

"And we're walking . . ."

To our amazement, he thought about it for only a moment,

then picked up his small hooves and followed. On his own. No carrot, no stick. Just followed.

I guess as long as he thought it was his own idea, he was willing to cooperate.

Flash stepped nonchalantly behind us the remaining distance, as if we were out on a Sunday stroll. Perhaps he knew it was simply time to go home. Or perhaps he was plotting his return. Whatever the case, we hurriedly jury-rigged the gate in place behind us, and Priscilla stopped to admire the strength and determination it had taken to break it down in the first place. "Wow, that guy sure found his passion. He knew what he wanted and didn't let anything stand in his way," she commented. "I'd never have believed it if I hadn't seen it with my own eyes."

Like he knew we were talking about him, Flash seemed to shrug his narrow donkey shoulders with modesty and lowered his head into the grass to munch away, his foray into romance over with for now. Beau trotted out to offer his opinion about Flash's escapade, barking his moral indignation from behind our legs, but Flash simply ignored the criticism.

Priscilla and I made our way back to the house for some sweet tea and air-conditioning, relieved to have Flash back in the fold where he belonged. I pulled two glasses from the cupboard, then found a pen and hastily scrawled "find your passion" on an old envelope that was sitting on the counter. I thought I might like to muse about it later, but of course I promptly forgot about it. For quite a while.

But the funny thing about writing something down, even if you forget that you ever wrote it, is that the message stays with you long afterward. The envelope eventually went the way of gathered trash, yet the *mental* note attached to it followed me around and turned up in odd moments. Middle of the night. Halfway through a shower. Driving to the home improvement store.

"Find your passion."

Flash had certainly found his passion. There was a sheriff's report (and a broken gate) to prove it. I'd pictured his midnight rendezvous with the pretty little mare as a humorous anecdote to tell at a party, an icebreaker of a story that was sure to get a laugh. Flash was exceeding our expectations as a conversation piece, and I felt really proud of him for that, even if the circumstances were a bit sketchy.

But that note stuck with me.

Did I have a passion big enough to pursue with the same dogged determination Flash had? It was kind of a daunting thought, especially when so much of my life seemed muddled and unclear. As I could see it, I had several passions, all competing for my attention and not necessarily working together in one beautiful, synergistic purpose as I imagined they should.

Perhaps making a list would help. I brought out my notebook, turned to a fresh page, and paused. Finally, I wrote,

My Passions — Rachel Ridge

(Always write your name at the top.)

1. Faith — my core beliefs

I put this one first because I figured that's what good Christians are supposed to do. I remembered sitting in Sunday school and seeing circles drawn on an overhead projector image, with the center circle being Jesus Christ, and the larger circles around it representing other parts of your life, almost like ripples. Totally made sense. *Yes, this should be the first thing I list, even though I sort of think it ought to go without saying.* But it would feel funny to leave it off. *Or would it?*

I imagined those circles again and wondered what would happen if I took faith out of the center. What would I put in its place? Suddenly, seeing life without a moral compass and an abiding relationship with God at its core looked like a hopeless abyss. If I thought life was muddled and confused before, now it would be completely impossible.

Truthfully, as of late it felt more like a *value* than a passion, but when push came to shove, if the definition for passion was something like "strong energy or emotion that compels you," then faith would qualify. I was still a bit unclear about how it should actually look (i.e., if I were truly passionate, shouldn't I be in full-time service?). But I kept it at the top and moved on to number two. Maybe this little exercise would lead me to the answer.

2. My family

This one was easy. I found this passion the day we brought our first baby home from the hospital and became a family unit. I lay on the bed next to the most perfect pink bundle I'd ever seen, and I knew instantly that everything was different. As I smoothed the tiny ruffles on the dress her daddy had bought her, I vowed to be the best mother I could possibly be. I would love and cherish her, lead and protect her—and the babies that would come after her—no matter what.

Passion burst into flame and colored every life decision afterward: where we would live, what we would do, what kinds of food we'd eat, how we'd spend our time and money. Parenting wasn't a hobby or passing fancy. It took center stage as a passion worth pursuing, even through the setbacks (like forgetting to pick up a kid from school on his first day of sixth grade, losing patience with whining toddlers and teenagers, and wanting to run out the door at times).

Deep in my heart, I wanted to make our home an unforgettable place. A place that would ground our kids for life, make them feel loved, and give them a sense of belonging. I wanted our home and family, however imperfect, to be a sanctuary.

3. Creating — making art and stuff

(I decorated this point with doodles for emphasis, and also because I doodle when I think hard.)

And here is where Flash's pursuit of his passion really spoke to me. It was on the level of that outside circle used in the overhead projector image, that part of me that looked beyond the "done deals" of faith and family and wondered about things like interests and purpose and, I don't know, *experiencing joy*. I thought back to seventh grade, when my journey to discovering a passion for creating art died a sudden death before it even had a chance to live.

∧ ∧

It was my first day of art class—the elective I'd been waiting for ever since seeing the thrown pottery jugs, papier-mâché figures, and charcoal still lifes on display in the hallways of my junior high. "Make Art," said the sign above them, and I knew in my heart that I was born to do just that. I'd always loved colors and nature and crayons and glue. To think I would finally get to take a *real* art class! I had already pictured a blue ribbon hanging from one of my paintings in the hallway and a write-up in the school newspaper.

We perched on stools, our easels arranged in a square facing a table in the center of the room. A large clay vase was placed on the table. We were instructed to pick up our pencils and draw the container without looking at the paper secured to our easels.

"This is called blind contour drawing," said Mr. Hastings, the art teacher. "It is essential to everything else we will learn in this class. Begin." He abruptly sat down at his desk, opened a book, and left us to our work.

All the other kids brought their pencils up and began to draw, steadfastly staring at the vase without glancing at their papers. I heard the sound of charcoal points on manila, stool legs squeaking on industrial tile floors, the ticking of the large clock above the door. And I froze. The vase swam before me. My heart began to pound, and I felt my skin start to flush. My hand shook as I looked at the lip of the vase and tried to make my hand follow its simple shape.

But I couldn't help it: I peeked at the paper beneath my pencil and was appalled at the misshapen form burgeoning there. I erased and started over, but the horrific mess was still visible, now half-smeared and half-erased. Walking to the supply area for new paper, I noticed the incredible success my classmates were enjoying in their very first attempts.

Twice more to the supply cabinet for fresh paper. Still a

mess. As the others began to finish their masterpieces one by one, the classroom chatter got louder and more distracting until I simply gave up trying to concentrate and pretended to join in the banter.

The bell rang, and the room emptied. I gathered my books and stood next to Mr. Hastings' desk. Perhaps if I could get a little help, or at least a quick pointer, I'd be able to figure it out. I looked at the collages displayed just over his shoulder and couldn't wait to move on to those! The way the colors and shapes melded together to create spectacular scenes made me practically giddy with excitement. But first, I needed assistance.

"Young lady," Mr. Hastings said as he scowled at me over his glasses in response to my request, "if you can't do this first simple lesson, then I suggest you drop the class. You have no business being here."

I felt my heart drop into my shoes. Embarrassed, ashamed. Mortified by his indifferent judgment. "But, I . . ." I stammered, but he was already back to reading, the conversation finished. I could feel my eyes fill up and the room tilt. With one last, longing glance at the collages, I closed the door—not just on the class, but on *anything* creative. Anything artsy. Certainly anything involving pencil and paper. He was right: I had no business being there. I was a failure before I had even started. I was crushed.

The vivid details of that moment, down to the smells of oil paints, turpentine, and pottery slurry, became fixed in my memory. I learned to avoid creative projects of any kind—and I watched from the sidelines as classmates made scenic sets for plays, history dioramas, and cool collages. I would instead focus my attention on home ec, which it turned out I was also terrible at. But it was the elective I took in place of art—so practical, so sensible—and I would not pick up a paintbrush until I was well into my thirties.

How I wish now that Mr. Hastings had taken just three minutes of his time to encourage me to stick with it. To tell me that the whole point of the exercise was not perfection, but *practice*. To gently say, "I see you have a hunger for making things. Let me show you what you can do."

It took me more than two decades to rediscover my childhood passion and reach a conclusion that he could have easily pointed out in those moments after class. "Make Art" means so much more than blind contour drawing. It means "Create Something Beautiful." There are hundreds of forms of art—most of which don't require pencil and paper—and unlimited ways to create meaningful, beautiful things that people will appreciate and treasure. But I didn't know that, *couldn't* know that, because the door was closed to me that day.

I lost something important in one single moment. A budding, vibrant light was snuffed out. And it took three kids, an overworked husband, and a desperate desire to find something I could enjoy for me to find it again. I signed up for a tole painting class in a local craft store, simply as a way to get out of the house for a couple of hours a week. But with one dip of the brush into paint, something in my soul sparked back to life.

And so I had found a third passion: "Creating Something Beautiful." Or as I liked to call it, "Making Art and Stuff." It was like coming home. I didn't plan on trying to make a career out of it. I just needed to hold things in my hands that I had made. That I had decorated. That I had made beautiful.

And it was wondrous.

^ ^

Whew. I took a break from all that thinking and went to the barn. Flash stood under the shade of the sloping roof like a donkey statue. Perfectly still, except for the occasional swish of that wispy tail. His eyes were half-closed and his ears drooped downward, indicating that it was nap time, no doubt his third of the day.

With a click of my tongue, his head came up and his nostrils began to work. Ears turned forward. He nickered softly. Flash waited for my approach, then slowly rubbed his head on me as I reached around to scratch the warm patch underneath his mane. The scabs from the barbed wire were still visible, reminders of his dedicated quest through fences for his mare. I could see why she'd come around and fallen for him!

Passion is like a magnetic force that draws others in. Its energy not only compels you to act but also elicits a response from everything around you. I pulled a few burrs from Flash's mane and looked into his brown eyes, still sleepy from his interrupted nap. He didn't exactly look like a magnetic force at the moment, but it was like he *knew.* His determination spoke volumes, and it made me start to filter my scattered thoughts into something concrete. Something that made sense and felt right.

There was one last thing to add to my list, but I didn't know quite how to word it:

4. Helping others find and create sanctuary

I started to realize that my struggle to find peace and beauty in the middle of all my busyness wasn't unique to me. Others craved the same things I did. It seemed like each project Tom and I worked on had an underlying theme—to create a sense of sanctuary for our clients through art and design. But there was more to it than that. Sometimes we could see that art and design were cosmetic Band-Aids for deeper problems: dysfunctional family structures, unbalanced value systems, too many activities, maxed-out finances.

You see a whole lot when you're in dozens and dozens of homes for extended periods of time, and some of it is heartbreaking. You see that a pretty mural can't fix a broken marriage, or prevent aching loneliness, or help someone sleep better at night. And I wondered if, in a roundabout way, God had put a passion for beauty in my heart for a greater purpose. More than just paying the bills. More than just a creative outlet. More than just making pretty things.

But for something eternal.

Eric Liddell, the Olympian who inspired the movie *Chariots of Fire*, says in the film, "God made me fast. And when I run, I feel His pleasure." I often felt a sense of God's pleasure when I painted, or when I began to write my thoughts down on paper and saw beauty unfold in my words. There was a mantle of peace and satisfaction that warmed me down to my toes and caused me to wake up each morning eager to get going, excited to see what the day would hold. I'd begun to see that I was *made* to create things, and that doing so was an extension of God's own character flowing through me. Feeling God's pleasure in such a simple way made me want to share it with others.

My love for art was quietly birthing a love for people.

"Find your passion." The scribbled words were more than a worthy goal. I could not have known, in my twenties or even in my thirties, how passion would find *me* instead. Sometimes it takes a circuitous route, back to your childhood, to remember what brought you joy—before anyone told you that you couldn't do it, or that you weren't good enough, or that it wasn't practical. Before that voice in your head told you to close the door and take home economics instead.

Sometimes you bump into your passion when you're looking for something else, and suddenly it all becomes clear when you feel God's pleasure as you create or give or learn. And sometimes you just have to break down some fences and bust some gates off their hinges in order to catch the prize on the other side. And when you do, you realize that discovering your passion isn't an end in itself, but the key.

The key to finding your purpose.

Find your passion.
Passion leads to purpose.

CHAPTER 6

Sure and Steady Trails

stood outside the stately door of the aging mansion and pushed the bell. The faint sound of Westminster chimes filtered through the panes of the side windows. *Longest door chime ever. I don't know how people stand it.* "Just a minute," came a voice on the other side of the door. The lady of the house jiggled the handle up and down as she struggled to unlock it.

The wait gave me a chance to take a breath and collect myself before meeting this prospective customer. I pulled my blazer down to straighten it and shook my bangs out of my eyes. *Inhale. Now exhale.* Our project with Bridgette and Steve had led to further work at the corporate site, but it had recently ended. Now I needed to fill our schedule once again. So here I was.

I took stock of my surroundings. The home, which had been featured in design magazines in the 1970s, was once a show-stopper in the midst of the old-moneyed part of Fort Worth. But forty years had taken their toll, and the old girl looked unfashionably shabby next to the sprawling new mansions that were going in nearby.

Peeling paint on the wood door and trim, along with sagging gutters along the roofline, made the house look tired, and even the stiff boxwood hedges felt out of touch with modern style. Still, this was exactly the type of neighborhood we liked to work in: It had people who appreciated fine things—and who had money to spend.

The designer on this project, who had put us in touch with the homeowner, was new to me. I'd never met him before, but I appreciated that he'd seen our work somewhere and felt we would be a good fit for his clients. He explained they were in the process of updating their home and needed us to provide some beautiful finishes for the kitchen cabinetry. "There might also be a few minor repairs," he said. And then he'd hung up abruptly after giving me the address. A little odd, but hey, I wasn't complaining.

I rented a shiny new car, impressive enough to befit the sales call.

"*Here* we are!" said the lady, finally throwing the door open, releasing a smoke-filled haze into the outside air. "Watch your step." She pressed her slippered foot over the threshold to keep it from popping up and took a puff of her lipstick-stained cigarette. It was difficult to tell her age, but I guessed, oh, mid-seventies, with a little bit of work done to put her squarely in her late sixties. "We had a guy working on this door, and he never came back to finish." She shook her head disgustedly. "You just can't depend on people anymore."

"I know, people these days, right?" I nodded sympathetically and followed her into the dim entryway. She scooped up her black-and-white shih tzu, who was barking and baring tiny white fangs at me in welcome, and pulled him in close to her flowing housedress.

"Now, before we get to those cabinets, I want you to take a look at this water-damaged wall and give me a bid on fixing it, then painting a mural over the fix to disguise it."

I heard her say this, but I could barely tear my eyes away from the scene in front of me. A multitude of bears—scores and scores of collectible teddy bears—lined every wall, step, piece of furniture, and bookshelf. Bears in wedding dresses, bears in overalls, bears reading books, big bears, little bears, bears in rocking chairs, bears in frilly Victorian outfits, bears with monocles, bears with baby bears. Bears and more bears. It was a veritable bear bonanza.

"I collect bears," the lady said modestly, pressing her jet-black hair into its elaborate updo. "And modern Asian art, as well as commemorative plates. And anything with elephants on it." She motioned, spokesmodel style, to the sunken living room, where her collections were displayed in massive, ridiculous vignettes of utter tastelessness. It was as if the Home Shopping Network had unloaded all of its unclaimed merchandise right there. I felt an involuntary laugh about to erupt, but I remained professional.

"Lovely, just lovely. Almost takes your breath away." I busily pulled out my measuring tape and got to work. All those glassy bear eyes watching, watching. My neck prickled. And I knew instinctively, even as I measured, that she only wanted a price from me and did not plan to have us fix the wall or paint a mural over it at all. *Tire kicker.* You learn to recognize them quickly. People who don't care that it takes hours to look at each project, come up with a solution, create a design and a sketch, then present a bid . . . all without them ever planning to purchase from you. Not that I mind—I'm just saying.

We made our way to the kitchen, where to my surprise the cabinetry was freshly finished with a Country French, antiqued treatment. "You want to change this?" I asked.

"No, just fix it," she replied. She pointed to a very small area near the sink that needed attention. "I keep calling the painter to come out and finish this, and I've just given up. Obviously, he is not a very dependable person." She launched into a con-spiratorial rant about how difficult it was to get anyone to do a good job, the way things used to be done, and how terrible it was that no one even answered their phones anymore.

"I'll have to prep the wood and match the paint," I said, interrupting her lengthy remarks and starting to feel just a teeny bit put out for driving all this way to bid on such a minor repair. "It's a very small area, but it won't be easy to get it to look per-fect." I'd have to recoup my time somehow.

"I know you can do it," said the homeowner. "I just can't trust anyone else." The cigarette glowed. "Now, you need to see the guest bath and tell me what you can do in there. The wall-paper guy didn't pull off all the old paper before he quit, and I wonder—you can just texture right over it and make it look really luxurious, can't you?" What was left of the gold wallpaper, with red-and-black flocking, burned my eyeballs with its groovy '70s pattern. It was hard to think straight. Perhaps the wallpaper guy had been overcome with nausea.

"What are your ideas?" she demanded. The dog in the crook of her arm quivered nervously with a continuous growl, chas-ing off any creative thought I might have had. *Easy now, Fluffy.* But I graciously spent the next fifteen minutes discussing ideas with her for the guest bathroom, which I knew was another tire being kicked.

My eyeball problem was giving way to a massive head-ache, but the tour was just beginning. From the guest bath, we trudged through strewn laundry to the master bath, where the plumbers had left their tools and everything, presumably for a lunch break. But that was two weeks ago. I began to see a pat-tern here. *No one ever comes back.*

My pounding head, the awful fluorescent lights, her gravelly voice going on and on about the plumbers . . . I zoned out for a moment or five, which was unfortunate, because I did not see the *other* shih tzu coming, full force, to attack the back of my ankle. *Ack!* I shook him off and tried to act casual about inspecting the bite mark. Bleeding! *Are you kidding me?* That wretched little dog had punctured a vein with his needle teeth. That's when I stopped pretending to smile and just gritted my teeth for the remainder of the tour.

Please, dear Lord, make this end.

But God, in His inscrutable wisdom, was clearly not interested in swift intervention. He was going to leave me hanging. On toward the master bedroom we went. I could hear children down the hall singing the *Barney* theme song and ventured some small talk.

"Oh, how sweet. Are those your grandchildren I hear?"

"No, not grandchildren," said my hostess. She flung open a door to a huge walk-in closet. "Parrots."

Three large gray birds, in three enormous dusty cages, all bobbed their heads, their beady eyes glued to a TV screen and singing with reedy voices, "I love you, you love me, we're a hap-py fam-i-ly . . ."

"They *love* this show!" she exclaimed. "I keep it on 24-7, just for them." I brushed a floating feather from my nose and instantly realized that someone had put drugs in my drive-through coffee, and I was hallucinating this whole thing. Suddenly, the singing parrots made perfect sense. Of course. That feather wasn't even real, was it? Hysteria bubbled up, along with a cold sweat. *So this is what it feels like to lose it. Bu-whahahahaha!*

If I had had plumber's tools, I would have dropped them and run, but instead I clutched my black satchel and snapped my notebook shut. I turned to make my exit, but before I could make a clean getaway, she kept the party going with one last item.

"I want you to meet my husband," she announced, and like a lamb to the slaughter, all I could do was follow helplessly to the next room.

"Frank! This is Rachel! Frank! This is the artist!" my tour guide rasped as we burst through the door. Shrouded in blue cigarette smoke, Frank, a shrunken little man, sat deep in the recesses of a faded floral couch, hooked up to an oxygen tank. The tank was at one knee, an ashtray on the other, just above a large leg bandage. He lifted his perfectly bald head in greeting and sputtered something unintelligible, his words drowned out by the *Barney* chorus and barking shih tzus. In that instant, I knew that I, too, would never come back.

"Ohmygoodness, look at the time!" I pretended to look at my watch and wheeled around. I limped back through the house on my one good ankle, dragging my bloody stump behind me, while the lady shuffled to keep up, explaining the problems with home health care in minute detail. Something about Frank's leg wound not healing properly, and would I take a look at it and tell her what I thought. My thought at that moment? *Why me?*

We made it to the door. Finally! But it wouldn't open. So I waited in desperation while she jiggled the doorknob for a full minute before releasing me from the netherworld of bears and disappearing workers.

Air! Fresh air! My rental car! *I take back everything I ever said about finding a quiet love for people.* My heart was a giant hole of nothing. Except fear.

And possibly horror.

I called Tom the minute I got out of the driveway.

"We are getting regular jobs," I said in no uncertain terms. "You cannot believe what just happened to me." I laid rubber on the road as I peeled onto the freeway. "Also, and I'm not joking, I think I may have been drugged."

My description of the event took most of the drive home. When I finally arrived, a shower removed the stale smoke from my hair. The clothes could be laundered. But I could not shake the nightmare.

The problem was, we needed the money, and I knew we had no choice but to go back. We'd have to work with shriveled-up Frank and the singing parrots, rabid shih tzus, and awful smoke. And all that talking! My head throbbed.

Tom guided me to the couch and handed me a steaming cup of tea, along with a square of dark chocolate (with sea salt and caramel—so healing). "Have this," he said, "and then let's get you into bed. There you go, baby." I looked at this guy who after twenty-five years of marriage knew I needed to hear that everything was going to be all right. "We can manage without this job," he lied. And I loved him for it.

∧ ∧

I slept off the dreadful experience (or detoxed?—whatever), and when morning came, Tom brought me coffee and handed me my shoes. "Let's get Grayson off to school and then go for a little walk." By now Meghan was in college, and it was easy to get one kid out the door with a sack lunch. This was good: I needed easy.

The air had just a hint of fall in it, and a slight breeze rustled the dry grasses in the field as we took each other's hand and slipped outside. Neither of us needed to say anything grand, which is one of the very best things about being together since forever.

We let ourselves through the gate and walked into the pasture, our steps instinctively taking us to one of Flash's trails. About twelve inches in width, the path was perfectly groomed by his set of hooves and just wide enough for single file. Tom dropped back behind me, our fingers releasing.

The trail meandered toward the barn along the fence line for fifty yards or so before dividing into two. One of the branches led on to the barn, while the other angled off across the field. We chose the one angling off and followed it around to where it intersected with another of Flash's trails. Taking a right, we headed through the back pasture toward the woods, our feet still following the furrow that was carved through the grass and tall weeds.

"I'll bet this place looks crazy from the air!" I shielded my eyes from the morning sun and looked eastward across the field. It was crisscrossed with his paths in some kind of pattern only a donkey could make sense of. Each corner of the field was connected by a trail, with intersecting, veering lines going this way and that. None was straight, but each was like a gently undulating, dry riverbed created by his moseying walking style.

"Hard to believe he can do enough plodding to keep these so well maintained," Tom said, admiring Flash's work ethic. "Look, this one goes from the woods to the barn, with exits in case he changes his mind!" The main arteries were well worn and deep, but even the secondary paths looked oft used.

We glanced up just in time to see Flash emerge from the woods, where he loved to sleep at night. True to form, he used the most direct trail route to reach us. We watched his hooves plod, plod, plod toward us and saw that they dragged a bit of dirt with each knock-kneed step.

Flash came to a stop by Tom, nosing his pockets for a treat. Tom produced a Tic Tac and palmed it for Flash's soft, thick tongue to grab, and we laughed when he drooled at its mintyness. We listened to him crunch it, the sound echoing in that big old head. Then I sighed and looked at Tom, not wanting to talk about that job but knowing we probably should. I wanted to quit this whole thing, so I said as much.

"Rachel, we aren't going to take that project, so stop worrying about it. We'll be fine. We've always said 'Not all business is good business,' and this is a perfect example. Something else will take its place. You'll see."

Tom threw an arm around Flash's neck and gave his friend a good knuckle rub on his fuzzy forehead. The donkey turned his head into Tom's chest and vigorously rubbed up and down, leaving a dusty print on his dark shirt. Looking over Flash's ears at me, Tom continued. "Besides, not to be corny or anything, but I think we just need to keep plodding on."

"Oh, ha-ha-ha," I laughed, holding my stomach in feigned mirth. "Aren't you clever!"

"No, I'm serious." Tom's smile became earnest. "We need to remember that we're in this for the long haul, and that the journey is just as important as the destination. Look at how far we've come and how many good things have happened along the way. Look at our kids, and how we're living here now, fighting for something worthwhile. Look at the fact that we're standing in a pasture with a donkey on a weekday morning, while the rest of the world is sitting in traffic to get to their desk jobs. We are doing something we love. Yeah, we've had our insane moments, but I wouldn't trade anything for where we are right now."

I looked around at all those trails, made one sedate step at a time, by a donkey who never really seemed to pay attention to where he was headed, and I considered what Tom had said. Maybe he had a point.

Plod, plod, plod. That was exactly what we were doing. Progress was so slow. It didn't appear like we were heading anywhere. Success was nowhere on the horizon, and our tempo seemed to drag. But *at least* we were moving. We weren't sitting still. We were taking steps, forming habits, creating lanes. And all those lanes were intersecting, weaving, making way for life to happen. It didn't all rest on one job. Hmmm.

We were walking now, single file again. Tom, me, Flash. You never really like to be the one right in front of Flash because he has no concept of personal space. He puts his nose right up by your back and playfully nibbles at your clothing as you move along. He really needs to work on that.

Just as I arched my back in anticipation of his nudge, I heard hooves pause behind me. I turned in time to watch Flash lower his nose to the ground. We'd walked directly through his favorite roll spot, where he loves to bathe himself in dirt. It's a wide circle, worn clean of grass and weeds, right down to the soft, loose soil beneath.

Flash's roll spots—hidden jewels in a pasture comprised largely of Texas blackland soil (much too clumpy) and limestone rock (not enough dust)—are well chosen for their quality of sandy dirt, and he enjoys the ritual of bathing in them like you can't imagine.

Now trancelike, with half-closed eyes and flattened ears, he circled several times, his muzzle leaving a groove in the fine sand. His front legs seemed to buckle, and with a deep exhale he lowered himself to the ground and kicked up a giant plume of dust with his back feet as he rolled over.

Belly up, he rolled from side to side in violent motions punctuated by gas and groans. He rubbed his back into the ground with relish and finally came to a stop with legs splayed out, tail rapidly sweeping the dirt. One more roll. He heaved a happy sigh and looked up at us over his dust mustache. I was ready to hear him say, "Thanks for waiting, guys. That felt great."

Flash threw his front feet forward and pulled himself up, covered in dirt from ears to rump, just the way he likes it. The layer of dust would help repel the flies and mosquitoes and protect him from the sun—important quality-of-life issues for creatures who, for obvious reasons, would have difficulty applying sunscreen or insect spray by themselves.

We continued on our way, finally stopping at the water spigot near the barn, where Beau was waiting for us. He'd opted not to walk with his rival, but he didn't seem to mind that we had done so. "I'll take you guys to the house," his expression said as he wagged the tip of his tail at us.

With his shoulder to Flash, his body language clearly excluded the donkey from the conversation. The two tag-teamed our walks, passing us off like batons, with Flash taking the pasture zone and Beau in charge of the yard. However awkward, it seemed to work for them.

Tom topped off the bucket beneath the faucet while the

sun warmed the four of us. I had never considered Flash to be a trailblazer, even though we'd seen him run with horses and romance a beautiful mare. He certainly had experienced some big, shining moments. But his characteristic gait was s.l.o.w. He didn't hurry, and he seemed to step methodically. He rarely even looked up as he ambled.

And it dawned on me then that there was something important in his trails. They were daily efforts that created structure and made pathways for others to follow. And maybe just as noteworthy, they intertwined to create an intricate pattern that didn't always make sense from up close, but could easily be seen from another perspective.

I did a mental flyover, imagining my life as Flash's. (I would definitely do something about the buckteeth and big-ear situation.) I looked down at my own pathways to see if I could find any patterns—any definitive trails that I could identify.

At first glance it looked just like Flash's haphazard pasture lines, but as I pulled my lens back further, I began to see how all those threads were interconnecting, moving, and weaving. Like an unfinished tapestry, with unraveled edges, but with the beginnings of something beautiful taking shape.

I saw how the path of my childhood as that awkward missionary kid had led to young adulthood and Bible college. And how the path of Bible college had led to meeting my husband and thinking we would be courageous humanitarians in some far-off corner of the globe. As twentysomethings, we just knew we would change the world with our zeal and dedication. *Jesus and us and the gospel!* But somehow life and kids and work had changed those plans, and the trail took an unexpected turn.

For so many years we felt that our path was "less than" those of more dedicated servants, who gave it all to follow higher callings. While we lived in suburbia and enjoyed the everyday luxuries of running water, flushing toilets, and Walmart, they were putting their lives on the line in grass huts somewhere. *Are we doing enough? Are we sellouts? Are we selfish to pursue a dream that uses our creative gifts?* We kept treading. Diapers, Sunday school, work, offering plate.

Faith had often been presented as an either-or proposition: Either you are a 100 percent willing vessel or a halfhearted church attendee. A minister or a pew sitter. A doer or a spectator. An on-fire zealot or a pallid Christian. There wasn't much middle ground to speak of. It took years of plodding to realize that there was, after all, *a place for us*, and it was not in a manufactured state of guilt, but in a grace-filled space within His care.

Faith, we learned, is not an occupation, but a lifestyle. It is a matter of the heart that encompasses everything. Step by faltering step, we had made a trail from the woods to the barn, from hyperactive duty to genuine worship. Circling around and coming back. From work . . . to grace . . . to offering.

Making dinner, taking kids to piano lessons, changing the oil. Finding that God is in our work and our play and our family. In our hockey games and Bible studies, our bedtime prayers and errands. He is in our sketches and paintbrushes and dreams. He is in our *showing up* each day and lacing up our shoes and being fully present in whatever situations we find ourselves. He is in our very breaths.

Walking, stepping, plodding. Doing the next thing.

From the weight of thinking we needed to have all the answers in our zealous youth, to the darkness of having none— not a single one—in our moments of despair. Like when we lost

Collin. Or when we had to choose which bills to pay. Getting lost, and feeling our way.

And one day, waking up to embrace the freedom of the mystery. Savoring the not knowing. Resting in faith. Being in awe of a God who sees and knows, and who waits. It all happens in such incremental moments, as you work out your life into some kind of reflection of Him in your everyday world. You are making trails, even when you don't know quite where you are heading.

And all the tangled knots, the hard places of your journey, become dots on the map. They are interspersed with the stretches of plains, the mountains, and the joyous milestones, all of it coursing into a magnificent pattern borne of slow steps and determined feet.

Each marker holds its story. "Remember that time?" you say, and you laugh or fade off into quiet reverie, retracing your steps and shaking your head. You see how each place you mark makes way for a new trail to be blazed. Yes, some of the trails peter out, and you have to back up and start over. Some of them are easier than others. And some don't make any sense at all, at least from your perspective. The point is, you are moving. Not standing still. You are putting one foot in front of the other, and as you do, somehow . . . God is there.

Step, step, plod, step.

He puts people in your path—like Priscilla, who entered my life with a phone call inquiring about a nursery mural, and who never left. With her endless encouragement and generous friendship, she changed my course forever. "Want to see a movie?" she'd ask, and it was like a lifeline when I was most lonely.

And Bridgette. Our Southern belle neighbor, who was ever growing on me with her "Well hi, y'all"s and her delicious gumbo that sometimes arrived outside our front door along with a kind note. She still called Flash THAT NAME, but it bothered me less and less these days.

Trail markers, northern stars.

Psalm 32:8 says, "I will guide you along the best pathway for your life. I will advise you and watch over you." How incredible to know that His hand is leading and His eye is watching over us. And Proverbs 16:9 states, "We can make our plans, but the LORD determines our steps."

As I waited for Flash's bucket to fill, I remembered the time I was at Chick-fil-A with Grayson on a particularly stressful day. We'd just left a dentist appointment that took forever and cost some exorbitant sum, and I was in a hurry to get back to work to make up lost time. I swung into the drive-through lane and placed our order for life-sustaining chicken nuggets, waffle fries, and sweet tea. The young lady on the other side of the intercom was incredibly polite, and I was even more impressed with her when we reached the window. She took my money, gave us our food, told me it was a pleasure to serve us . . . all while employing such intentional eye contact with me that I made particular note of it to Grayson.

"See, now *that* is how teenagers should interact with adults. Making eye contact is so important! I hope you'll remember to do that, Gray. You'll go far in life if you do." Hey, you can't let a teachable moment go to waste.

As I handed Grayson his food, I happened to catch a glimpse of myself in the rearview mirror. *What?* Suddenly I knew exactly why the girl at the window had looked at me so intently. The left lens of my sunglasses had fallen out—I'd been talking to her with only one tinted lens!

"Good grief, Grayson! How long have I been driving around like this?" I demanded of my son, whose mouth was already stuffed with waffle fries. I pointed at my missing lens and glared at him. Through his chipmunk cheeks, he mumbled something about not being able to see that side of my head from the passenger seat. Glancing over, he nearly choked as he spit out the fries and howled in laughter. *Not a shred of compassion, that kid.*

How could I not have noticed that I was missing a lens? How could I not "see" something so conspicuous? I realized later that I was just too close to the situation—literally. (It didn't help that I was distracted and worried at the time.) But my mismatched lenses were only too obvious to someone looking from another perspective. Looking out from my broken viewpoint didn't reveal the truth; it was only from a distance that reality was clearly seen.

I wondered, how often do we fail to see the big picture? How often do we look at present circumstances and make decisions based on what we see and feel today? We forget that it's in the walking, in the daily tasks, that the work of grace gets done. Sometimes we just have to step back in order to see it.

Flash's coarse hair along the cross on his back already felt hot in the morning sun. He plunged his lips into the cool water and drank deeply from the full black bucket. His sturdy neck rippled with each swallow, his nostrils opening wide, then closing. He finally brought his head up, water dribbling from the corners of his mouth, and looked at me. Through long eyelashes, his darkly rimmed eyes held my gaze. He blinked and brought his wet nose up to my face to sniff my cheek.

In that moment, I was filled with gratitude for this homeless donkey and for all his crazy trails. And I thanked God for all the times during my journey that I'd begged for rescue, for change, for intervention—and God in His inscrutable wisdom had left me just where I was.

Because it was in the waiting, and the wondering, and the plodding that I had to do the most trusting. And found the most grace.

You can't always see the destination, but perseverance will take you there.

He is with you each step of the way.

Always.

Be a trailblazer.
Persistence makes pathways for grace to follow.

CHAPTER 7

A Matter of Paternity

Can I get you a cup of coffee? No? How about some lemonade? It's sugar-free." Bridgette ushered me into her ultra-stylish home office for a design meeting, but first, her Southern hospitality took over. She adjusted the round glasses on her nose and smiled. "You just set right here and let me get you something." Bridgette said "here," like "heeah," which always made me smile.

"No, thank you. I'm fine." I declined the refreshment and sat down. My Midwestern sensibilities and Norwegian roots required me to refuse all first and second offers, on account of that's how we do it. It goes against our stoic grain to put anyone out. We don't want to be a bother. Really, we don't. We couldn't.

Unless, of course, they make a third offer.

Then we can consider it.

"Water, then? It's no trouble," Bridgette insisted. "But the lemonade is delicious, and I've already got it made." The pitcher was hovering over the glass, Bridgette's eyes on me, awaiting my response. I was no match for this "steel magnolia" and gave in.

"Well, since you've already made it . . ." Gracious acceptance was my only recourse in this situation. She poured it over ice (again, too much trouble, but she already had ice out) and set the glass down on a coaster in front of me.

"How about some cheese and crackers?" I could see that Bridgette was going to make this difficult.

"Oh thank you, but, no. I just had a late lunch and couldn't eat a bite." I held my hand up in polite refusal. But she was already bringing a small tray with an array of cheeses, a selection of crackers, and clusters of grapes.

"You've simply got to try this Brie," Bridgette said. I noticed that it was topped with some kind of raspberry marmalade, oozing down the sides in a decadent display of epicurean goodness. This lady didn't play fair.

"Oh my. That's too pretty to eat. I might need to just Instagram it instead." I could feel my mouth watering. Raspberries are my favorite. Also any kind of cheese.

Bridgette took a cracker and dipped it into the soft wedge to tempt me. "It's from Costco, and we bought so much, more than Steve and I could possibly eat. Please help us eat some of it up!"

As I thought about it, lunch *was* several hours ago, and it only made sense to have an afternoon snack. And she'd gone to all this work to put the tray together.

"I really shouldn't." I was still reluctant but hated to insult her hospitality. "I'll just have one or two bites."

Heavenly. She had so much of it, maybe three or four bites, or ten, would take some off her hands. It was the least I could do.

I decided that only classy people happen to have Brie (and gourmet marmalade) on hand for last-minute meetings. Bridgette somehow made me feel like I was doing her a favor by eating as much as I could. I don't know if Southern women go to school to master the art of persuasion or what, but she had a summa cum laude degree in it. I could learn something from her.

Bridgette had a new client who needed artwork in his luxury condo in downtown Dallas, and she wanted to go over the design plan for the whole space before we were scheduled to go to the location together later in the week.

I sipped my lemonade as I took out a notepad and started looking at the paint and fabric swatches she had chosen while piped-in music drifted through the eclectic office that looked part downtown loft, part Texas country, and part urban renewal. Galvanized metal blended seamlessly with stained concrete floors, modern lighting, sleek workspaces, and well-chosen antiques. I loved the old wrought iron stair rail and sliding barn door. Fabulous touches. A library of architectural books and samples filled an entire wall, and a massive bank conference table, used mainly for Ping-Pong, held center stage. You couldn't help but admire the panache with which Bridgette and Steve merged their work and home lives.

Over the months of working together on various projects, I had come to appreciate Bridgette's talent for seeing possibilities in everything. *Oh, she's very good.* Case in point was this office. She and Steve had recently bought the property that Flash's cow friends had lived on and moved from the cottage near us into a barn. Seriously, who moves into a cow barn? Well, only people who can reimagine, repurpose, and reuse anything and everything to convert it into an incredible home and office space. What was once just a big metal structure had become a functional and inviting living and working environment that anyone would envy.

It was no wonder Bridgette was successful. I could see that now. She could take any old item and make it into art or a functional piece of furniture. She and Steve could design a whole building on the back of a napkin. It almost made me sick, but I was comforted by the fact that they loved what *we* could bring to their projects artistically. And as it turned out, we worked well together.

"Say, have you seen how big the dark mare next door is getting?" Bridgette finished fussing over the refreshments and pulled up a chair. "When do you think her baby is due?"

"I have no clue," I said. "But her belly is huge! It looks like she might explode any day."

It was true. Maria, the beautiful ebony horse that Flash had crashed through fences and gates for, was definitely expecting a foal. There could be no doubt. We watched her girth expand from week to week as she went from sleek vixen to big mama. No longer trotting around the pasture with her band of friends, she now lumbered slowly, as if mindful of the new life inside her.

Flash had not made any more attempts to break out, but he lingered daily near the back gate and nuzzled with her when he could. It was a sweet sight, but boy, we hoped he was not the party responsible for her ballooning weight and thick ankles. The band of horses in the pasture included two stallions, so chances were good that he was off the hook on this one.

"Any idea if *Hay*-soos is the father?" Bridgette shot me a wink. She'd heard about Flash's rendezvous with the cutie, and it was something of a famous joke by now.

"Bridgette, you *do* know his name is Flash, don't you?" I laughed. This had gone on long enough.

"Of course I do, but that's just my lil' pet name for him." Doggone it, she looked so sincere, I couldn't be mad about it anymore. Besides, it really didn't matter what she called him. It only mattered who owned him, right? He belonged to me, so what difference did it make? None whatsoever. This conversation was far easier than I had thought it would be. Why had I feared it so much? Maybe I was growing or something.

"From the size of her, I'd say it's more likely that one of

those big stallions over there is the stud," I said. "I sure hope so. The last thing we need is a custody situation." With each day that passed, I worried that our neighbor would show up with papers and a paternity suit. He'd probably have the sheriffs with him and everything. *Please, Lord, let this foal be a horse and not a mule.*

"You'd better keep your fingers crossed," Bridgette cautioned with a smile.

"Believe me, I am. Anyway, we're planning to have Flash 'fixed,' so we should be able to put this behind us." I grimaced at the thought of the impending operation as I picked up my pen and notebook.

We focused on the business at hand. I looked at the plans and took notes, squinting my eyes and staring off into the distance as I imagined the options for the space. The biggest challenge was to create an art piece using a specific shade of brown for a twenty-foot-high wall. Because elevators and hallways would interrupt the space, something on such a massive scale would need to be installed in pieces, yet feel seamless. Between the two of us, we had made a good start on the overall project. But I knew it would take a really special idea for the owner of the luxury apartment to say, "Wow! That's perfect!"

After our meeting, I walked home, a flowering perennial from Bridgette's garden perched atop my stack of samples. Not a bad commute, when the only other traffic is cottontail rabbits who scurry out of the way.

I stepped carefully over the cattle guard between our properties, and Flash met me by the gatepost. "Hey there, Donkey Boy." I set my things down and reached out to scratch under his scruffy chin, working my way up his face to his ears. Dust from his last dirt bath wafted up into the air and settled back down. "So what's that baby gonna be, huh?" I asked him, but he didn't say. Instead, he turned his body around until his rear end was facing me, and then backed up so I couldn't miss his rump.

"Nice," I said. "You won't talk to me, but you'll let me scratch your rear. I get it." Flash might be an animal of few words, but he certainly knows how to communicate when he wants to. And he loves having his backside—the only place he can't reach with his teeth—rubbed. He turned to look back at me, with a "well-what-are-we-waiting-for" expression, and relaxed his back hoof in anticipation of a massage.

So I obliged, chuckling out loud at the incongruity of standing in a field, rubbing a dusty donkey's backside after a fancy business meeting to discuss a luxury condo design over Brie and crackers. Flash had really come a long way since he first arrived, so scared and broken in those early days. I thought about how he hadn't wanted us to touch him, how he had shied away when we came to tend to his wounds and had kept a wary eye out for any sudden movement.

Looking over Flash's hips to the field beyond, I remembered how Tom had set up that camp chair in the middle of it. He'd been so patient, pretending to ignore Flash by engrossing himself in a book, or by "bird-watching," all the while allowing the donkey to become accustomed to his presence. Flash had inched his way closer and closer, fearing mistreatment, but receiving instead gentle words and kind handling. First, a rub on his nose. Then, a hand on his neck. He had stood, trembling, as Tom felt his way down the coarse hair, across his chest and over his shoulders.

His fear had gradually given way to trust, and he repaid

Tom by becoming his loyal companion. He followed him every-where, always loitering near Tom's work area, curious about anything he did. Affectionate and playful, Flash loved to lean into him, nibble at his water bottle, and sniff his pockets.

Flash would have let me scratch his bum all afternoon, but I had other things to do. With a final dusty pat and a hug around the neck, I headed back to the house.

∧ ∧

"Here's what I've come up with," I reported to Tom after seeing the condo later that week. "How about a Venetian plaster finish on two-foot square panels, mounted in a grid pattern over the whole wall? We could use a stencil technique to emboss some Latin phrases that would run up and down the panels to visually connect them." I believed it solved every issue beautifully, and I was pretty proud of it.

"Hmmm . . ." Tom thought about it for a few moments and then said slowly, "I think we can do better." He took out a piece of graph paper. "I like the idea of panels, and if I've done the math correctly, it will take forty-five squares to cover that mas-sive wall. But what if we emboss individual words that describe a 'Life Well Lived' on each panel? To really knock it out of the park, we could use a different language for each word, which would reflect both the travels of the client and his values."

Yep, it was better. In fact, it was brilliant. We presented the idea, and the client loved it.

With approval granted for the design, Tom perfected the plaster finish technique, while I researched words to describe elements of a well-lived life. Now *this* is the kind of art I adore, because it combines the aesthetic with a meaningful message.

It made me pause and reflect on what a well-lived life really looks like.

Is it about success? Relationships? Experiences? Character? Faith? What would make someone say about another, "This person really knows how to live life well"? The concept for the art had been a simple one, really. But its profound questions resonated with me as I pondered the characteristics that have marked humanity's aspirations throughout history.

In the end, we used words like these:

Love
Honesty
Friendship
Generosity
Kindness
Faith
Patience
Gratitude
Peace
Hope

Each element of the art piece required time. Time to decide on just the right word, time to translate it into another language, time to choose a font, time to lay it out, time to apply it to each panel. I found that when I handled a word like *love* or *gratitude* or *joy* that long, I meditated on it throughout the day, even when I wasn't working on it. I felt intentional with my energies as I worked, talked with the kids, did laundry, and bought groceries.

Can a person have joy while scrubbing a toilet? Can you

experience love while spreading peanut butter on a sandwich? Gratitude when your head hits the pillow? I was beginning to think that perhaps living well—in any circumstance—might be possible, if your heart is in the right place.

^ ^

The condo project would take several weeks to complete. Bridgette and I conferred regularly and took a couple of shopping excursions to purchase decor. Our common mission was so enjoyable that sometimes I even forgot we were working.

Imagine *me*, laughing it up with the CEO of a prestigious design firm! Yet here we were, having a ball digging through thrift shops and antique stores as we sought treasures for our client's home.

One day, Bridgette called with some exciting news.

"Did you see the new foal?" she asked. "I just caught a glimpse of it out my window!"

"No!" I answered breathlessly. "It's here? What does it look like?" Then worriedly I inquired, "Does it look like a mule?"

"I couldn't tell. It was staying pretty close to its mama."

I threw down the phone and ran out the door, grabbing Grayson by the arm as I passed him in the breezeway.

"The baby! Maria's had her baby!" I huffed.

Now outside, we opened the gate and took off across the field toward the fence, with Beau joining in to see what the fuss was about. We arrived at the back gate and climbed onto the lowest crosspiece to get a good view. Leaning forward into the sunlight, we could see the horses grazing midfield. I spotted little legs hidden behind the black mare as she nibbled grass. Everything was quiet except for the rustle of leaves stirred by the breeze.

Move aside, Maria! We willed her to turn. We could see a small tail swishing near her, but the baby's form was obscured by her frame.

At Grayson's whistle, the horses' heads came up and turned toward us. They paused; then the leader, a large copper stallion, started forward. The rest followed suit, with the mare and her baby bringing up the rear. *Still can't see!*

Fifteen yards now, nearly close enough to view. *Almost . . . almost there.* The group stopped just beyond us, clumped together around their newest member, before slowly fanning out. *C'mon, c'mon . . .* We held our breath. At last the mare broke from the group and gently nudged the baby at her side, as mothers often do . . . as if to urge him, "Say hello to these people, Son." He tumbled forward, blinking at us in surprise.

Finally, our first glimpse of the foal.

Oh honey. Just look at you.

Our eyes took in the perfection before us, and we exhaled, the air passing slowly through our lips as we took him in.

You look just like your mama . . . and your daddy.

You're dark brown, with unmistakable markings.

A distinct gray muzzle.

Softly circled eyes.

Ears that are much too long.

Your mane is all bristly.

Your tail is funny.

Your head is just a little too big.

Darling baby, you are a mule! *A beautiful little mule.*

And your daddy is that smug-looking donkey in the next pasture.

One look was all we needed. The strong family resemblance

vanquished all doubt. We had a mule baby on our hands. And Flash was the father.

The foal's long legs carried him toward us before he suddenly realized that his mother had stopped several feet back. He leaped as if his legs were made of springs and quickly hopped to her side. Turning shyly to look at us, his eyes were inquisitive and eager in a face that was a perfect blend of Flash and his ladylove.

"Come! Come here," we called to the group as they made their way through the grass to our open hands. Then the foal and his mama hung back, reluctant to get too close. It looked like the baby was just a few days old, its legs far too long for its body, but otherwise robust and healthy. What a miracle he was! His tiny tail bobbed back and forth as he decided to remain out of our reach.

Oh, he was cute. And now I figured we'd get a visit from the sheriff's department, demanding that responsibility be taken. There was no denying the truth before us: Everything on the inside of that baby showed on the outside. He had donkey blood in his veins, and it endeared him to us more than any thoroughbred breeding could have.

We slipped to the fence whenever we could to watch his progress as he filled out and grew into his long legs. Always bashful around us, he never ventured far from his mama's eyes. Flash's *laissez-faire* parenting style left the day-to-day care to the ebony mare while he observed from a distance the darling baby that bore his markings. He looked on indulgently while the mule leaped over imaginary obstacles and kicked up his heels with rambunctious energy. Maria seemed quite content with this arrangement, looking after the needs of her growing foal without interference from the opinionated donkey next door.

Everyone who saw him seemed to fall under his charm, including his mama's owner, who joined the ranks of those smitten by such a perfect mule. Much to our delight, he decided to keep him after all. We could continue to see him anytime we wanted.

∧ ∧

The summer flew by as we worked on the luxury condo. Bridgette and I had one last meeting to wrap up the details. We sat in her office amid stacks of files and samples and her colored markers and architectural plans. I felt fortunate that someone of her professional stature would be willing to take me under her wing and teach me how to take things further.

I'd learned so much already: how to create design boards, how to make presentations, and how to read construction documents. I was picking up the terms: FF&E (Furniture, Fixtures, and Equipment—my first!), RFQ (Request For Quote), charette (an intense collaborative session), lights (windowpanes), chamfer (to round off), and ingress/egress (in/out), to name a few. I was out of my league but trying hard to look as pulled together and confident as Bridgette.

I looked at the punch list in my hand. "Tom and I will be on-site when the chandelier gets installed," I told Bridgette. "I think that's the last thing to be done." The condo had turned out even better than we had hoped. It was thoroughly urban-contemporary, with a touch of Texas rustic flair. The art piece that graced the massive wall was a stunning focal point for the entire space, and it was gratifying to see how it had all come together.

"Great." Bridgette checked off her notes. And then there was a little pause. "So . . . Rachel, how do you do it?" she asked, returning her orange marker to its case and resting her chin in her hand.

"Do what?" I was puzzled by her sudden question.

"You know." She seemed to be searching for the right words. "How do you . . . have such a beautiful family in the middle of everything you are doing?" I looked up and saw a serious expression on her face. "I mean, you and Tom have so much going on, and yet you make it seem so easy to love each other. You have good relationships with your kids, and you're so at peace all the time."

Bridgette stopped for a moment and then added slowly, "Steve and I used to drive past your house when we lived in the cottage, and sometimes we could see inside your windows. It always looked so warm and wonderful in there. It's made me wonder how you've done it."

I dropped my pen with a clatter, speechless at this revelation. But it was her next statement that nearly made me fall off my chair.

"You seem so perfect, and it's hard not to be intimidated by you."

Intimidated? By me? I couldn't be hearing right. This, from the beautiful, impeccable, successful Bridgette. The woman I idolized as having it all, who could eat raspberry jam–topped Brie and crackers, balance her business and personal lives, and still maintain a twenty-four-inch waist.

In a moment of clarity, I realized that Bridgette saw all the good and pretty parts of my life, not all the ugly ones I was trying to hide. I had convinced myself that she noticed my mom jeans and our old truck and my lack of professional polish, so in my insecurity I put up a wall that projected I had it all together.

I didn't want her—or anyone else—to see my struggles and failures, so I kept her at arm's length and tried to look self-assured and impenetrable. Safe—from a distance.

This was my *modus operandi*: friendly, but friend*less*. Except for Priscilla, there were very few people I let in. Few saw the real me, with my flaws and wrinkles. It was a pattern I'd started as a gawky teenager, so insecure and snaggletoothed and unfashionable next to the popular girls and successful athletes in high school.

Back then I'd learned to be funny and gregarious, hiding my introverted self behind a confident mask so that I'd fit in without risking rejection. It was history repeating itself—only now instead of cheerleaders, I substituted other women I deemed better, smarter, prettier, and more accomplished. Bridgette was all of those things. Best not to let her see what's on the inside.

But the charade suddenly made me feel lonely.

Bridgette's question opened my eyes. I had been jealous of her perfection, and all the while she was envious of mine. Yet neither one of us was truly what the other thought. Both of us had false perceptions based on our own insecurities. Sitting here, our elbows nearly touching on the table, my defenses began to melt, and I realized something I hadn't recognized before: We were no longer just two women from opposite backgrounds. We were in a sisterhood of fear and comparison that kept us in a place of mistrust and loneliness. We held ourselves up to one other and always came up short. Each of us taking our weakest points and comparing them to the other's strongest. Each of us hiding behind our strengths and wearing them like armor.

"Oh, Bridgette, if you only knew the truth—how much I've struggled to be a good mom and have a good marriage with the challenges we face. Maybe I made it look easy because that's what I wanted you to see. The truth is, I fail way more often than I succeed. I don't multitask well, and I'm always juggling more than I can handle. My pants are hemmed with duct tape. I can never find matching socks. I'm disorganized and distracted." I sighed. "All this time, I've been intimidated by *you*. I was convinced I could never measure up to how smart and competent and talented you are."

Vulnerable, exposed. But finally genuine and real. I had put my heart out there, and now I held my breath. *Please don't hurt me.*

To my relief, she cradled it gently.

"Wow." Bridgette pulled the word out like soft taffy. "I think we have a lot to learn from each other." I nodded, swallowing the lump in my throat.

"Tell me more about that duct tape trick." She chuckled. "I've got some pants that need hemming."

Twilight was falling as Bridgette and I stepped outside onto the porch. It was time for me to head home. The late spring air was cool on my skin, belying the warmth that usually ushered itself in this time of year. I could see the horses grazing in the adjacent pasture, just a few yards north of Bridgette's house. Their soft nickers and blowing sounds told me they were thinking about heading back to their own barn for the night. Just then, a little set of long ears came forward to check out the movement in the yard. *Little baby. How I adore your mixed-up gene pool.*

Bridgette pulled her beaded scarf around her shoulders and pointed out a lone bloom amid the spent greens of earlier flowers. "Look at my last purple iris. All the other ones bloomed weeks ago, and this one finally opened up yesterday! It's all by itself. Idn't it gorgeous?"

"Beautiful!" I admired the frilly petals of the last iris, standing so tall and proud. "Gotta love the late bloomer." We laughed.

And then I turned to her and whispered, "I think I'm a late bloomer, Bridgette. I feel like I'm late to everything . . . late to figuring things out, late to friendships, late to finding my whole purpose in life." I took a breath. "But maybe that's okay if what I'll get in the end is a spectacular finish like this."

"Well, me too," Bridgette said. "Me too, girl. Better to bloom late, than to never bloom, right?"

We smiled at each other in the gathering darkness and high-fived over our heads, fingers catching as our hands dropped. How could it have taken me so long to see this jewel of a friend right under my nose? Perhaps she'd been offering her friendship all along, and I was too busy being stoic and self-sufficient. Too worried she'd discover my flaws and reject me. Declining the first and second offers on account of that's how I do it. Circling, fearing mistreatment, but receiving kindness instead. I had been so foolish.

Thank You, God, for third chances, and oftentimes more. And for Southern steel magnolias like Bridgette.

She had helped me understand something important. A life well lived is about character—that's true. It's when what's on the inside—love, generosity, faith, joy, and all that good stuff—shows on the outside. But it's also about the people whose lives you are a part of. Those you let in . . . those whom you allow to see your most vulnerable part—the side that isn't perfect, doesn't have it together, doesn't have everything figured out. It's when you quit comparing and stop hiding that you start to bloom.

I saw that character really means *nothing* without people to share it with. When it comes down to it, character is really only as good as the relationships around you. Honesty, love, generosity, and truth must have an object, or they remain theories rather than becoming realities in our lives. Proverbs 22:1 says, "Choose a good reputation over great riches; being held in high esteem is better than silver or gold." It's in your friendships, your community, and your family that character makes all the difference.

Maybe a life well lived is about wearing your heart on your sleeve, *your donkey soul on the outside,* just like our little mule next door, with his distinct light muzzle and softly circled eyes. He couldn't hide his shady paternity, even if he wanted to. But because of it, we love him all the more. *Ears too big, tail too odd . . . oh dear baby.*

It's letting the love and the fear, the joy and the sorrows, the confidence and the insecurities—all of it, every bit of it—show without shame. It's reaching out and learning to trust in the kindness that's around you, and allowing others to know the real you.

And that's when genuine love happens. *Better late than never.*

Wear your donkey heart on your sleeve.
A well-lived life is an authentic life.

CHAPTER 8

When the Rain Stopped

Drought. The year Flash arrived, Texas was hit hard by its worst dry spell since the 1950s. Ranchers were forced to sell off herds, and farmers lost entire crops from the lack of rainfall. Reservoirs were hitting rock bottom, exposing old tires and radiators in their fissured lake beds. It seemed that on every street corner and in every barbershop, coffee shop, and convenience store, casual conversation was marked by weather speculation.

"It's the La Niña effect," a wiry rancher told me over his Styrofoam coffee cup in the church foyer. "That's when the colder air and water in the Pacific cause drier conditions in the central plains and southwestern parts of the country. If we could just get that jet stream to move . . ." He explained that what we really needed was El Niño—the opposite of La Niña—to dump boatloads of rain on us.

Others were certain that sinister conspiracies were at work.

"Definitely the government," said a friend who was known to get inside information from Internet sources. "Well, not exactly the government. It's a secret organization, which is run by the government, to control radio frequency waves in order to change the weather." She elaborated at length on the high-altitude chemical vapors intentionally created by aircraft to alter weather patterns worldwide. Interesting. While this theory didn't explain the purpose of such nefarious governmental interference, it did make for lively discussion.

"Global warming," said another friend. "The greenhouse gases are ruining the planet. Just look at the pollution in Asia and you can see why we are suffering."

Still others proclaimed the drought to be the result of righteous judgment, a serious accusation against the state that regards itself as the buckle on the Bible Belt. This one seemed curious to me. Perhaps instead it was our self-righteousness—and not the outright sin and debauchery more prevalent in other geographical areas—that was to blame. Still, it was probably a good idea to do some soul-searching anyway. The governor called for statewide vigils, and people everywhere prayed for rain. We needed it badly.

Flash showed up just as rainfall totals were starting to plummet. By the time we realized the drought wasn't going anywhere, he was part of the family, and no matter what it cost in hay and care, he was here to stay.

He was the only one who seemed oblivious to the troubles around him, and I loved hanging out with him as the sun would set on another arid day. I brushed his sleek summer coat and applied fly repellent. Picked dirt out of his hooves and carefully cleaned around his eyes. It seemed Flash suffered from the same allergies that we did, and his eyes would get watery from dust and pollen. Flash's contented demeanor and quiet appreciation for the tender care always brought me a sense of calm as Tom and I continued trying to patch together a living and finish raising our kids in the midst of the Great Recession.

You had to hand it to Flash: He maintained a busy schedule. If he could have typed up a daily to-do list, I am certain it would have looked something like this:

1. Wake up among the cedar trees.
2. Enjoy the morning quiet.
3. Wander to the back pasture.
4. Follow the trail to the barn and check on breakfast situation.
5. Eat hay.
6. Solve world problems.
7. Nap.
8. Check resident mesquite trees for leaves.
9. Find delicate flowers to nibble.
10. Mosey to front pasture.
11. Scratch body parts on fence posts.
12. Socialize with neighbors over fence.
13. Munch on tree bark and weeds.
14. Stand near bois d'arc tree and wait for someone to pick up fruit and throw it to me.
15. Bray. (For best results, do this without warning.)
16. Nap.
17. Check on "people activity" near gate.
18. Loiter near barn.
19. Take a dirt bath in favorite roll spot.
20. Poop in designated piles. (Do several times a day, not particularly scheduled.)
21. Bird-watch.
22. Call it a day.

Flash's days were so full, it's a wonder he fit it all in.

After checking on the water level in his bucket and finding Flash finishing up #2 (enjoy the morning quiet) and starting on #3 (wander to the back pasture), I packed a sack lunch and grabbed my earbuds so I could head to a mural project. Tom loaded my ladders and paint supplies. He would spend the day working with his father on a little side business that brought in some extra income. The day promised to be an interesting one, as I'd never painted a scene on a wall of a room that housed an indoor swimming pool and felt excited about the prospect.

"Remember, Lauren and Robert and Meghan and Nathan will be home for the weekend," Tom said as he kissed my forehead through the open Explorer window. "Try and wrap it up early so we can order pizza and get a movie going."

"Can't wait," I said. Nothing sounded better than a weekend of comfort food and hanging out together. Maybe I could get the mural laid out and the underpainting done by the end of the afternoon.

Ignoring the check-engine light that had been lit up on the dashboard for weeks, I put the Explorer into reverse. A loud squeak emanated from the front end as I rolled backward. Well, *this* was new. My excitement for the day disappeared in an instant. I hit the brakes, and Tom and I grimaced at each other as our eyes met.

Well? my face said.

No time to look at it, his expression replied.

My eyes narrowed. *I hate this bucket of bolts.*

I know. He shrugged in sympathy, palms raised. *Me too.*

"Come around the house and park in back, next to the yellow Jag." My client's sultry voice oozed through the entry speaker as the heavy iron gate swung open. I pulled through the arches onto the expansive property and found a spot to park near the fleet of vehicles in the detached six-car garage. No matter how slowly I crept along, that squeak from the Explorer echoed off the courtyard walls as I rattled the vehicle into place. Lovely.

A yellow Jaguar, a blue Mercedes, a HUMMER, a convertible BMW, and a black Lexus were neatly lined up and polished in their spaces. *I'm so glad I got a car wash on the way—not that it makes much difference.*

The homeowner was the wife of a man who had acquired his wealth in the oil business. As we headed for the pool, she pointed out all the treasures she'd amassed from her overseas travels.

"You've probably never been to China, but I fell in *love* with Asian arts and crafts and brought some large pieces home with me. They cost a fortune to ship, but they're worth it." Her monologue was punctuated with odd inflections that felt like tiny pinpricks under my skin, and we were only minutes into the day.

She introduced me to the other service people on-site: the car detail guy, the cleaning lady, the window guy, the fireplace guy. I quickly discovered that she'd hired me as much for conversation as for painting. Unfortunately, I had not included "talking" in my estimate, so I was quite anxious to stick to the part where a paintbrush was in hand. All the kids would be home tonight!

There was not a minute to spare. I surveyed the scope of the project while looking over my shoulder as she ushered me along. Because first I would need a tour through the new east wing and indoor tennis courts, apparently to properly understand the feel of the home.

Finally we reached the end, and I was dismissed to begin my real job. "I'll let you get to it," she said with a wave of her hand. "I've got some online shopping to do in the other room."

The humid pool room was also home to an indoor garden. My mural would cover one of the walls, to give the illusion that an Asian "garden" continued on into the distance. Crammed with tropical plants, moss-covered rocks, and imported statues, there wasn't one level spot on the floor for my ladder. No place to set my tools. *Dear me, it's like a sauna in here.* I could feel a trickle of sweat make its way down my neck, and I knew my work was cut out for me.

As I unpacked my supplies, it was hard to shake that check-engine light and the humiliating squeak that had announced my arrival at this sprawling North Dallas manor. *I should be grateful for this project, but* man! It was tough to feel thankful after parking next to that yellow Jag. And all those comments that made me feel subservient. . . . I didn't know what to make of them, but they didn't help my mood. I was irritated.

Plugging in my earbuds, I tuned my iPod to worship music in hopes that it would improve my outlook. Listening to Chris Tomlin sing "My Chains Are Gone," I felt my pulse begin to subside to a normal level as I focused on the words and let the melody wash over me. I pulled out my sketches, already soggy from the humidity, and began to plot the mural design onto the wall.

Around lunchtime, my stomach was rumbling and my arms were aching when I heard a distant, muted pounding on a window. I turned on my unsteady ladder to see the lady mouthing something urgent to me and pointing to the door that opened into their game room. I removed my earbuds and climbed down as she went around to open the door to my sauna.

I stepped into the air-conditioned room in a cloud of moisture and caught a glimpse of myself in the mirror above the bar. *Oh for crying out loud. No!* My hair was stuck to my head like a greasy squirrel, mascara circled my eyes and ran down my cheek, and a green mustache graced my upper lip where I'd smudged paint. I looked like a Goth-inspired bag lady. And I was pretty confident that my deodorant had failed. It was the full package of Awful.

My client, on the other hand, smelled of freesia and oil money. In her manicured fingers was a catalog of the latest Mercedes models, which she laid open on the table next to us.

"I desperately need your help," she implored. "You have an artistic eye. I can't decide which Mercedes to buy: the classic dark-gray sedan or the hot little red convertible. Which do you think makes the best statement?" She blinked at me with her flawless makeup and waited.

I looked back at her with my raccoon eyes and my drippy hair, clenching my paint-covered fingers behind my back.

And I felt about an inch tall.

I was angry. I felt belittled and small and ungrateful. I was sweaty and bitter.

Um, have ya seen my awesome vehicle out there? Do you really think I'm qualified to tell you which car makes the best statement?

How about the one that doesn't squeak? Yeah, that one. Pick that one.

But I pointed to the red coupe with my knuckle and heard myself say, "Oh, take the red one! It's sporty and flashy and fun!" Did my laugh sound natural and light? Because I really wanted to sound natural and light.

The rest of the conversation blurred, along with the final hours of roughing-in the painting. As I threw my brushes and tools together to go home, she insisted that I take everything out again to touch up a furniture piece she needed for a party that weekend. In my mind, it was another strange stab to put me in my place and keep me longer than I wanted.

Squeaking home (without air-conditioning, I might add) in the red Explorer that made a *real* statement, I lashed out at God for His lack of care. Weeks between projects and then to get *this* one, working for someone with a sense of superiority? I knew the economy was hurting everyone, not just the farmers and ranchers and artists, but I expected a little better treatment here. I was sick of this recession. I was tired of cutting expenses, beaten down by that orange light blinking at me. And my hair still stuck to my head, although now matted into a crispy mess. If ever I needed those highlights, it was now. It's just that there was never quite *enough*. Never enough money, never enough time, never enough success, never enough of *anything* to go around.

When I finally arrived home, I turned off the engine and sat in the driveway for a moment. Flash was at the fence to greet me, sides heaving as he aired up for a loud bellow. *Not now, Flash. Spare me.* I sighed through puffed cheeks but got out of the car to see him anyway. The kids were waiting inside, but I needed a few moments to decompress—and hey, why not get blasted by a donkey foghorn while I was at it? I covered my ears in anticipation.

Flash's lips pulled back and his head came forward as he released the bray in an explosion of sound.

HEE-haw, HEE-haw, HEE-haw!

He subsided momentarily, then let forth again. *HEE-haw, HEE-haw, HEE-haw!*

"Good to see you, too, buddy." My shoulders were slumped in defeat, but sadly Flash is clueless when it comes to reading body language and paid no attention to my need to regroup.

He looked expectantly at me, then pointedly at the green horse apples on the ground near my feet. I noticed he'd positioned himself strategically near the bois d'arc (pronounced "bo-dark") tree just outside his fence. Most people call this kind of tree a hedgerow tree or horse apple tree because of its odd lime-green fruit, which look like oversized, pebbly tennis balls.

They're rock hard and worthless to humans, but horses and donkeys *love* them. Flash has perfected the art of eating one, which requires holding it against the ground with his mouth while biting off a hunk with his teeth. He then chews the sticky mouthful, with green slobber dribbling out, smacking his lips with relish.

Ahem. Rachel, look at me. Yes. Now look at the ground right there. He cocked his head, and his eyes sent invisible arrows to the fruit. I could not miss his intent.

Obediently, I picked up a horse apple and chucked it over the fence to him. It rolled to a stop near his front feet. His head lunged and he dug into it greedily, the juice squirting out as he bit down. I leaned against the tree and watched him chew the woody pulp with his eyes half-closed in delight. He polished it off in two more chomps and immediately implored me for more. A fresh one crashed to the ground with a thud, so I picked it up and held it just beyond him.

"What? You want this, huh? Huh?"

I couldn't help but smile a little at Flash's expression. His lips are so nimble, I swear he could pick a lock with them. He raised one side of his upper lip and flared his nostril, as if he knew I was teasing him. A swift nod of his head told me to get serious and hand it over.

"Okay, okay. Here you go." He took it from my hand and set it down on the ground with his teeth. Then, like the gentleman he could be, he brought his head up to say thank you. I rubbed the insides of his ears with my fingers, and he was only too happy to put off eating until the attention was over. I looked around at his barren pasture and marveled at how he managed to thrive with so little grass growing from the parched ground.

It's remarkable, really. Flash finds edible delicacies everywhere. He eats weeds that would insult horses, and he favors dry native grasses that even cows turn up their noses at. Made for the desert, the donkey is undaunted by drought—a natural browser who chooses leaves, bark, thistles, and brush when easy grazing isn't available.

I love watching Flash single out the specific plants he likes, no matter how small, and remove them from the surrounding growth with the skill of a surgeon. He selects blades of grass, bites them in half, and eats his favorite parts, like a connoisseur of vegetation.

Flash finds particular delight in the leafy fronds of mesquite trees that grow in and around his pasture. Somehow he is able to avoid the gigantic thorns as he grasps a small branch with his teeth, like a Spanish flamenco dancer with a rose. Then he slides his mouth down to the end, stripping the leaves as he goes along. You'd think he was popping caviar into his mouth, he enjoys it so much . . . with nary a scratch ending up on those big lips.

Between his daily to-do list, his appetite for weeds and

leaves, and the servings of hay in the barn, Flash was living like a king. Well, I was glad *somebody* was around here. What a character.

With my mood lifting, I gave Flash a farewell kiss on the nose and joined the family inside. Lauren and Robert; Meghan and her new fiancé, Nathan; and Grayson all cheered as I walked in the door.

"*Now* the party can start!" They knew how to make me feel good, and I shed the last vestige of bitterness over my day as they enveloped me in warm greeting.

^ ^

The morning coffee gave off its life-sustaining aroma as I puttered around the kitchen in my robe. Pizza boxes littered the counter, along with the dishes that had been left in disarray the night before. None of us had wanted to miss the movie by taking time to clean up. I'd enjoy a cup of coffee before the crew awoke and before embarking on the cleaning effort.

My cell phone interrupted the quiet moment. So early on a Saturday? It was Bridgette, calling from her family home in Louisiana, and something in her voice sounded off.

"What's going on, Bridgette?" I asked, and I heard her take a shaky breath on the other end.

"Rachel," she said. And I knew instantly that it couldn't be good.

"I found a lump."

The words no one ever wants to hear.

The words no one ever wants to say.

A lump? Please, God, no.

My heart stopped, and I reached for the kitchen counter as my knees buckled. "No. *No!* What? How? Bridgette, are you okay?"

"They are doing a biopsy, and hopefully it's nothing. It's probably nothing, right? But I can't tell Mama yet because of her heart condition, and I don't want to tell my kids until after I know something for sure." Her voice wobbled. "I just . . . I just wanted you to know. You're the only one outside my family who I can call right now. I need you to know what's happening. I need you to pray."

Tears of fear and anger. Not Bridgette. Not my steel magnolia. Not this woman who had given Flash a different name, who shared her perennials and forged an unexpected friendship with me, the girl who didn't think she needed a friend. I refused to believe it.

But the cancer was real. And it was big. And there were surgeries, and chemo and radiation. She was sick, and her tiny figure got even tinier as she lost weight during her treatment. Her hair came out in clumps until she shaved it all off.

And through all of it, Bridgette was the one who was strong. Tom and I brought chicken dinners and flowers and made cards, but it felt so meager in the face of something this enormous. Mostly, we prayed. *Please, dear Jesus. Heal her. Do a miracle.* We wanted an instant zap. A beam from heaven to take away the cancer in one big blaze of glory.

But it seemed that her miracle would unfold in the long, slow journey of modern science and hospital waiting rooms. Her recovery would eventually be found in the care of excellent doctors and nurses and drug therapies. In the end, we didn't care what form the healing took, and we felt grateful for each step toward remission.

In the middle of her months of treatment, we started a new

design project together. I watched as something like light emanated from Bridgette in a way I'd never seen before. There she stood, bald as a billiard, conducting meetings and drawing up plans and executing her designs. She'd clutch a chair during a hot flash, peel off a layer of clothing, wipe her neck, and just keep going.

She surrounded herself with family and friends and drank in every Scripture about healing. She danced with Steve on the jobsite floor and wore bright, gigantic earrings and colorful scarves. It was like she squeezed all the goodness of life into each precious day. She had never been more beautiful or radiant. And I loved her all the more.

"Rachel, you cannot believe how liberating it is to be completely bald," Bridgette told me one day. The wigs that she'd so carefully selected, and was so certain she'd wear, made her scalp itch. She said she felt fake when she wore them. So she decided to meet the world *sans* hair. "I never realized how good it would feel to let go of all that pride that was so wrapped up in my hair, and to just say, '*This* is who I am.'" She threw her arms wide and raised her face skyward, open and free, thankful for life, and for breathing and loving. She grabbed my hand and whispered, "God is so good."

Bridgette, like Flash, found a way to thrive in the midst of her drought. It put my problems into a new perspective. Both Bridgette and Flash seemed to have discovered the secret to living in abundance, despite the odds against them. Watching them, I knew I had some soul-searching to do.

"Stand where fruit is falling," I wrote in my journal that summer. I didn't know why that phrase caught in my mind, but it did. Those worthless horse apples that littered the yard—they became treasures to a donkey stuck in a barren landscape. And the weeds and leaves that everyone else overlooked—they were sustenance and life to him. Somewhere, somehow, in the middle of drought, abundance could be found. And I had nearly missed it, because I was looking for easy grazing.

I thought back to the yellow Jag client, the lady who had everything money could buy. Now that I was past feeling like a feverish, greasy squirrel and had invested in some waterproof mascara, I could think a little more clearly about that whole incident.

From the moment I'd driven through the imposing gate and pulled up next to the fleet of luxury vehicles, I'd focused on all the shiny material things in front of me. I was occupied with thoughts of orthodontia, car repair, and the cost of hamburger. *It's ground meat, people. Not steak!* I certainly wasn't living in abundance, but I suddenly realized that the wife I so envied, who felt the need to jab the less fortunates at every turn, wasn't either.

Had I glimpsed disappointment in her face—there, amid her beautiful surroundings? I wondered if the stepchildren she mentioned resented her, and if she wished her husband were home more often. She filled her days with shopping, rearranging, lunches, and parties, but beneath it all, there was fear that everything would disappear with the onset of age and wrinkles.

She was grasping at a lifestyle that should have brought peace, but instead it only heightened her insecurity. People who have enough never need to point out everyone else's lack. I could see that now. Abundant living must be about something deeper and more lasting than a bank account.

I headed to the pasture with my notebook and Bible, this time wanting to get to the heart of this idea of living in abundance. The dried mesquite pods that swayed in the hot wind sounded like Mexican maracas as I dusted off the green camp chair near the fire pit.

Right on cue, Flash approached and nuzzled my shoulder, then lingered nearby to keep me company. He delved into the small stand of trees and found a branch, shoulder height, that he could rub against. Working clockwise around his frame, he scratched every inch at that level before moving on to a taller branch for his head and neck. I guess this time he actually read my body language that said "I'm deep in thought" and figured he'd take care of his own needs.

I felt like the person in Proverbs 6:6 who was told, "Go to the ant . . . consider its ways and be wise" (NIV). Only I was going to the donkey, the ancient animal who happened to show up in many significant stories recorded in the Bible, as well as in the lives of this average family in Texas. *Was it coincidence?* I began to think maybe it wasn't. So how was it that Flash always had enough? What was his secret of abundance?

My eyes found Habakkuk 3:17-19, which describes a desolate scene:

> Even though the fig trees have no blossoms,
>   and there are no grapes on the vines;
> even though the olive crop fails,
>   and the fields lie empty and barren;
> even though the flocks die in the fields,
>   and the cattle barns are empty . . .

Wow, now *that's* drought. Sounds familiar.

> *Yet* I will rejoice in the LORD! [emphasis added]
>   I will be joyful in the God of my salvation!
> The Sovereign LORD is my strength!

He makes me as surefooted as a deer,
able to tread upon the heights.

Clearly, these verses are saying that joy and strength are found in God. Even when there is drought. Despite all the odds against them. In the face of despair. In the midst of your troubles. Okay, I could see that. *But how, exactly, does it work?*

A hot breath of wind curled the pages, and I smoothed them back down. Flash abandoned the self-serve scratching post and stepped close to my chair to sniff the book in my lap. I knew he couldn't read, but he pretended to anyway, his lips moving ever so slightly as if forming the words. I nudged him and asked, "What do you think, Flash? Is there an answer in there?"

He flapped his ears as if to say, "See for yourself. I can't do your work for you." At this, I pushed his head out of the way to look for a clue—and found it next to the "yet."

"Yet I *will*" told me what I needed to know.

I must *choose* it.
I must choose to rejoice.
I must choose gratitude.
I must choose to look to Him for strength.
I must choose to find fruit.
It is a matter of my will.

Ah.

This whole abundance thing starts with a decision to see the goodness around you and give thanks in your circumstances. First Thessalonians 5:18 says, "No matter what happens, always be thankful, for this is God's will for you who belong to Christ

Jesus" (TLB). It is in being fully present and fully engaged in the act of gratitude that joy can be released in and around you. Intentional thanksgiving is when you humbly receive what God graciously gives you and offer praise to Him in return, creating a grand circle of abundance.

Flash's to-do list is a simplified form of abundant living. He awakens each morning under the cedars and enjoys the gift of a new day. He moseys to the barn to see what has been provided. He looks for sustenance in unexpected places. He eats hardship for breakfast. He takes the things that are disdained by others and relishes the nutrients he finds. He asks for help from his community. He strategically positions himself for fruit. He lives in the moment. He poops conscientiously. He is grateful for simple pleasures. He chooses contentment.

And none of it is dependent on material wealth, or even health, as Bridgette showed me. She wrestled with the fear that came with the cancer, the weakness that followed the surgeries, and the exhaustion that radiation brought. And through it all, she found a way to see God's love in every step of her journey. She chose to treasure the gifts that accompanied the pain: the gifts of friendship, of family, and of daily graces. She even treasured the gift of freedom that came with her loss of hair. If that's not living in abundance, I don't know what is.

"Stand where fruit is falling" means this: "Position yourself where the good stuff is." Find the goodness and get there. *Just get there.* Because the goodness can only come when you're standing in the right place. . . .

I was starting to see the picture now. All of it is a decision. A choice to savor the grace of each moment and to experience abundance in the very act of gratitude.

I smiled as I thought of Tom taking my hand in the Home Depot parking lot one Tuesday afternoon and twirling me around and into a dip, for no reason at all. I thought of the kids and the pizza boxes, and piling in on the couch to watch movies and enjoy popcorn and milk shakes together. The squeaky front end of the Explorer announcing my conspicuous arrival at the yellow Jag mansion.

The honor of bringing baked chicken to Bridgette, who beat her cancer in high style, with her big earrings and irrepressible joy. The laundry and the bills and the dailiness of living, all mingled with the sparkles of evening fireflies, the morning coffee, and the camp chairs set around a fire pit, in a pasture where a donkey lingers.

You can stand where fruit is falling. On a hot August day, in the middle of drought, there is fruit that looks like worthless, hard-as-rock oddities of nature.

But it is so. Much. More. Than that.

It is the "yet" that sets joy atop a mountain of trials, and plants a flag of triumph there for all to see. It is the "even though" that sees past the empty stalls and dried-up fields and vines with no grapes, and sets its sights on a Savior who is always enough. It is the arrow that points to a God whose lavish grace gives and sustains life, and makes our feet dance upon the heights. It is the "I will" that chooses daily gratitude, and a heart that rejoices in His loving-kindness.

It is the secret of abundance.

Stand where fruit is falling.
The secret of abundance is in choosing gratitude.

CHAPTER 9

Barn Management

Your donkey is being a pest," Tom announced as he wiped his boots on the mat outside the kitchen door. "I can't get anything done with him looking over my shoulder so closely."

He stepped inside to wash up for lunch, frustrated that he hadn't gotten more accomplished on his barn remodeling project. He was converting two stalls into an enclosed workspace, and the morning's goal of laying a subfloor had not ended well.

I finished making a ham sandwich and opened a bag of chips. It hadn't escaped my notice that Tom had referred to Flash as "your donkey." *Uh-huh.* It's just like when one parent tries to shift the responsibility for discipline to the other parent. "Your son needs a good talking to." Or "Your daughter exceeded her texting limit." It's a subtle way of saying, "It's your turn to take care of this."

So, like every good parent, I got defensive.

"He's just curious, that's all," I said, excusing Flash's behavior. "You know he has to see everything that's going on. Plus, you're his leader, and he wants to be near you, so we should cut him some slack."

Don't get me wrong; I love that donkey to death, but I'm not taking the fall for any mischief he pulls in the barn.

"Well, he's no help whatsoever," Tom replied. "He hasn't done a lick of work since he's been here, and now he's keeping me from doing mine." His expression was one of mock disgust, and I detected indulgence in his voice. Big softy.

The fact is, Flash's personal work ethic does leave something to be desired. As impressive as his pasture trails are, they are about the only thing he's actually worked at since he arrived on our doorstep. But even *that* job is suspect, because we know there is food, or water, or a roll in the dust at the end of each of his paths. Not exactly what you'd call an altruistic effort.

No, I'd say that Flash thinks of himself as more of a supervisor than a worker. He definitely has management potential— I'll give him that much— although his people skills could use some help. He's a bit of a micromanager. And this is where we run into problems.

Case in point was this stall-to-workspace project in our barn, where the only door in this open-concept structure is for the tack room. The stalls are partitions, and the remaining area is covered but open to the pasture, giving Flash free access whenever he wants. Flash took it upon himself to personally oversee the entire renovation by standing directly in Tom's way at every turn.

He staked out the area between Tom and his tools, turning his head this way and that to inspect each hammer blow and wood cut. Swishing his tail and sniffing the box of screws, he knocked over the drill and stepped on the measuring tape. He lapped at Tom's water bottle and devoured the crumbs from a granola bar. And he farted way too often for Tom's comfort.

"Back up, Flash ol' buddy." Tom pushed him a step backward so he could reach his carpenter's level. Flash complied for a minute but was simply incapable of letting Tom do the next part on his own. Crouched over the floor joist to secure a new beam into place, Tom felt Flash's warm breath near his ear. The "supervisor's" muzzle hairs tickled the nape of Tom's neck as he measured. Not satisfied with his vantage point, Flash inched closer and hung his head over Tom's shoulder for an even better look. He offered his opinion with a slight shake of his lips. *Up a little higher on the right*, he seemed to say.

"Hey, how am I supposed to get anything done with you resting your head on me?" Tom reached an arm around Flash's neck and gave his nose a rub with the other hand. "What I really need you to do is carry a load of lumber from the truck to the barn." At such a ludicrous suggestion, Flash cocked his ears sideways with a look that said, "You're kidding, right?"

Tom eased his body from beneath Flash's head and stood up to get some supplies that were stored in the tack room. Opening the door to the narrow room and stepping inside, he found what he needed on the back wall.

Clunk, clunk.

Clunk, clunk.

Before Tom had a chance to turn around, four hooves had stepped up into the space behind him, the clunks echoing on the wood floor.

"Seriously, Flash?" Tom slowly turned, arms up over his head in the tight spot. Flash's body trapped Tom against the shelves, his forehead planted into Tom's chest. "I'm just getting an extension cord. You don't need to check up on me." He pressed on Flash's shoulders to get him to back out. There could be no turning around in there. He'd have to exit rump first.

Flash didn't budge. He just stood there in silence, blinking straight ahead. Clearly, he didn't trust Tom's selection of the twenty-foot cord. The utter burden of having to manage *every single move* that occurred around here made him sigh in deep resignation. Oh, the incompetence.

"Okay, you win. I'll grab the fifty-footer." Tom pulled the longer cord from the shelf and slung it over his shoulder. "Happy now?"

Reluctantly, Flash clunked backward, off the step, and into the open barn, knocking over a can of paint in the process.

"So much for being a service animal." Tom teased him with an elbow nudge, righted the can, and returned to his work. "You're absolutely worthless."

A service animal! Hey!

Inspired by Tom's suggestion that Flash might be able to carry a load of lumber, I embarked on some research to see just what a donkey could be capable of. To my surprise, and despite Flash's less-than-stellar example, I learned that donkeys are the number-one service animal on the planet.

Millions of donkeys around the globe do the hard work of hauling, plowing, carrying, milling, and pulling—jobs that people in developing economies rely on for their livelihoods. Donkeys are the John Deere tractors, the delivery vans, the family cars, the Ram trucks, and the lowly servants of the Third World.

Photos of donkeys laden with heavy loads and looking as if they had stepped from the pages of ancient literature filled my Google searches. It's as if time stood still for these gentle beasts of burden, and for the people in poor countries whose daily survival depended on them. Even here in America, donkeys are still used for riding, packing, and working.

Flash had no idea how easy he had it on our little acreage, what with his supervisory position and all. It was high time he learned what he was made for.

∧ ∧

"Mom, our friend Barbara is not doing well." Meghan tucked a stray red curl into her loose bun and bit her lip in worry. "They've brought hospice in to take care of her."

"Oh, I'm so, so sorry." I knew how difficult this was for Meghan and Nathan, who were now married, and their small community of friends. Nathan had befriended Barbara several years earlier when she would regularly sit in his table section at the restaurant where he worked during college.

Barbara was a lonely, physically challenged woman who needed someone to talk to and occasional help with errands and tasks around her apartment. Nathan, Meghan, and their friends had made themselves available to assist her when she needed it.

Barbara had no living relatives, and as her health began to decline, she came to depend on the weekly rides to the grocery store and coffee shop that the friends provided. In a short period of time, she became unable to work and was forced to live in a small hotel room, nearly destitute. At fifty-five, Barbara had aged beyond her years, and she was understandably bitter over her situation.

"Well, she . . . can be *difficult*," was how Meghan described her once. "But that's just Barbara. She's had a hard life." It was a kind way of saying that Barbara was not an easy person to love. She had long lists of things she wanted help with, but she wasn't always appreciative of the assistance she received.

By now, the group of friends had graduated from college and embarked on new careers. It became more challenging to meet her needs amid their growing responsibilities, and Barbara herself was more cantankerous than ever. Daily chores became unmanageable. Tasks like getting dressed, taking care of personal hygiene, and preparing meals were nearly impossible for her.

The friends juggled their own busy schedules and did their best to help Barbara with the most basic needs. Meghan arranged home health care, scheduled social visits, and even assumed official power of attorney, all as she started her first year as an elementary music teacher. We worried that it was too much for such a young woman to handle.

But Meghan and her friends were all in. They had taken on Barbara as a personal mission of mercy—and found themselves loving this difficult woman whom the world had all but forgotten. When she could no longer get out of bed, the state stepped in and moved her to a nursing home. And now, hospice had arrived.

Meghan began to make arrangements for Barbara's imminent passing, but there were questions. When a person is a ward of the state, who takes responsibility for her body when she passes? Where is she buried if there is no one who will visit her grave? What do you do with her belongings and personal treasures when there is no family member to take them? Who will perform a funeral for someone who cannot get out to attend church? And who will come to a service for someone who lived in such isolation?

There was no one else.

This group of friends would see Barbara through to the end.

Sadly, she died as she had lived—alone, except for the company of the hospice nurse since no one else could get there in time.

Barbara's memorial service was held in a tiny chapel on a university campus. Tucked under gigantic oak trees, the stone structure was hushed as a handful of people—the former college kids—filed in. A table in the foyer held carefully displayed photos and mementos from Barbara's life: her favorite coffee cup, the hat she liked to wear, a poem she loved.

Meghan had collected personal items from her hospice room

and agonized over what to keep. There was no family member to give anything to. No relative who would treasure a memory or smile at a faded photo. There was just a small group of young people—a little oasis of love in a life that had been hard.

Tom and I sat in the second pew and watched as one of the girls set up a floral arrangement she'd made; another handed out a printed program. Then it was time to begin. Two of Barbara's friends led the sparse assembly in songs with a guitar accompaniment. There in that simple chapel, "Amazing Grace" had never sounded sweeter, resonating on the stone walls and then fading into the winter air. Meghan gave a eulogy, and Nathan spoke. Thoughtful words, carefully chosen, filled with affirmation and honor.

We were there to remember someone whom the world out-side had already passed by. A life that had become very, very small at the end. A life that, some would say, held little mean-ing. But somehow, this assembled group of grace-filled friends had validated her existence by serving her in love. They had gone out of their way, making personal sacrifices and giving of themselves, because they believed that serving is what they were made for. Barbara's life, and death, mattered to them.

Amazing grace! How sweet the sound . . .

For days afterward, we went about our work with quiet hearts, deeply impacted by the love we'd witnessed at the simple service for this woman. It felt sacred, and words seemed frivo-lous, unnecessary. I filled Flash's hayrack with his daily ration, held his face in my hands, and scratched under his chin. He seemed to understand my reluctance to talk and sighed gently as if to fill the spaces left empty of my normal chatter.

That same week, we were stunned to hear the news that

two residents of our town—Chris Kyle and his friend Chad Littlefield—had been killed while they were trying to help someone in the community. Our local area was grieving the loss of these outstanding men.

Suddenly for us, Barbara's passing was thrown into stark contrast with Kyle's death. The famed US Navy SEAL who had become a national hero was the epitome of service to his country. His bestselling book and movie, *American Sniper*, details his life and commitment to freedom. Self-sacrifice, dedication, honor . . . his life was marked by these attributes, and it touched everyone around him, including our own family. Kyle had given a couple of talks at Grayson's high school, which was also Kyle's alma mater. Kyle had inspired the kids to become the best they could be and to serve their country unselfishly.

We couldn't believe someone who had achieved such greatness could be from *our* obscure Texas town. He was just a guy from the class of 1992 who'd found what he was good at—and went on to become the most decorated sniper in American history. He was a larger-than-life hero.

And now, his life had been cut short.

The funeral was televised from Cowboys Stadium in nearby Arlington, Texas, and we sat at home in tears as we watched the ceremony. A flag-draped coffin, carried by Navy SEALs, slowly made its way to the front and was set amid dozens of floral arrangements. The familiar strains of "Amazing Grace," sung by country singer Randy Travis, echoed through the enormous structure. In moving tribute, decorated generals spoke, friends offered eulogies, and his wife, Taya, shared her heartbreak.

The following day, we joined tens of thousands of mourners lined up along the highway between Dallas and Austin to pay our respects. Facing a chilling rain and gusty winds, we held a flag as the long procession of government dignitaries, Navy SEALs, police and fire departments, family and friends all passed by in silence. Helicopters flew overhead as news crews captured the scenes of enormous flags hung across bridges and overpasses, and the people, young and old, who turned out to honor the slain hero.

The passing of these two individuals within such a short span of time could not have been more striking. They were so very different . . . and yet there was a strand that connected them—a common thread beneath the surface that haunted me. One, who was honored by thousands, was remembered for his unparalleled service. The other, who was honored by a tiny handful, was remembered for what she could not give. One served many; the other was served by a few.

Two people.

Two funerals.

Two gifts of service.

It got me pondering.

Though one gave and the other received, it was *service* that gave each life meaning.

I needed to talk things over with Flash, and he sensed my readiness to discuss what had transpired. As a member of a breed made for service, I figured he might have some insight, despite his lack of actual experience. Pulling up a chair in the barn on a cool February afternoon, with a Styrofoam cup of coffee in hand, sounded like just the ticket to enlightenment.

As Flash nosed his way toward me in hopes of receiving an apple slice along with the conversation, I was reminded of the donkeys who had turned up in my Internet searches—the ones who looked like they'd stepped off the pages of ancient history books. Saddled with loads piled high, pulling heavy carts, or carrying sun-wizened men in turbans, their nimble hooves seemed to echo through time and land—*plop*—right in the Old Testament.

The Bible records donkeys as being valuable assets. (No pun intended.) A man's worth, back in the day, was measured in land, cattle, sheep, goats, and donkeys. A bit more cumbersome than today's "what's in your wallet" method of transactions, donkeys were a hot trade commodity, and it was always a good idea to have a couple dozen in your back pocket, so to speak. I can only imagine women approaching their husbands about some new drapery fabric, on sale for a limited time, as traveling merchants came through town.

"Honey, it will only cost three donkeys! That's a whole donkey off the regular price!"

Twenty-five percent off has always been great incentive to buy. Some things never change.

I started noticing every mention of donkeys in scriptural text. Listed in terms of wealth, ceremonially set apart, ridden by historic characters . . . donkeys are woven into the fabric of biblical life. A tool for everyday work, a prop in a narrative story, a symbol for royalty. From Abraham to Jesus, donkeys served. One even spoke out loud!

The donkey who bore Mary, the mother of Jesus, is one who served in complete obscurity. In fact, he is not even mentioned in the Gospels. But the eighty-mile trek from Nazareth to Bethlehem would likely only have been possible with the help of a sturdy donkey, and tradition tells us that Mary made the uncomfortable trip atop the back of one such animal. I imagine Mary's backache was no different from mine, making a walk to the pantry for a midnight snack nearly impossible, let alone a journey by foot to a distant town. A ride on the bony back of a donkey would have been a welcome alternative to a painful pregnant waddle through the difficult terrain.

As I looked at Flash, I pictured that Christmas donkey in my mind. When Joseph saddled him up and tied extra padding down for Mary's ride, the donkey could not have known he would be making the trip of a lifetime. When he stopped to graze by the side of the road and was urged onward by an anxious husband, the animal couldn't have imagined that his journey would end in a stable filled with holiness, angelic choirs, oblivious cattle, and a baby wrapped in a handmade blanket. Well, maybe he'd have guessed about the "oblivious cattle" part. I mean . . . *cattle*, right? But he could not have known that the entire course of history was turning a page, *and he was part of it.*

No. He simply walked.

He did what was asked.

He followed Joseph for eighty miles. His halter, made of rough twine, probably rubbed his nose as he carried the coming Savior and His young mama. This donkey trodded along the rocky trails, the cobblestoned roads, and the dusty paths to ferry the precious cargo that would change the world.

He did what donkeys do best: He served.

How just like God to use another donkey, thirty-three years later, to bring the Savior-King through Jerusalem on another amazing journey. Handpicked by Jesus, this donkey could not have known that the job for which *he* was chosen would bring grace and forgiveness. He carried Jesus through the uneven streets, stepping carefully over cloaks and palm branches, to the final, climactic scene of Redemption.

Hailed, celebrated, famous for his role, this Palm Sunday donkey is forever remembered whenever the story is told.

But he did nothing out of the ordinary, for a donkey.

He walked.

He did what was asked.

He simply did what donkeys do best: He served.

Jesus' remarkable life was bookended by two donkey rides. Imagine that. The first took place in obscurity, to a tiny stable in a little town. It ended with a baby's cry, some swaddling clothes, and a gaggle of shepherds who came in from the fields for a glimpse of the Promised One.

The last took place amid cheering throngs and against a backdrop of Passover and deep social unrest. It brought all of human history to a single, pivotal point on the time line of eternity. This ride ended with a cry from a cross—"It is finished!"—and an empty tomb.

I was struck by the poetic drama of it all. Amazed by the vivid realization that God uses ordinary means to do extraordinary feats. There, in the barn with my coffee and the donkey who thinks he's midlevel management *at the very least*, I was bowled over by the service these lowliest of creatures had rendered to bring about this story. It's as if God chose to unfold His plan using the most humble tools available so He could reach humankind with His gift of grace.

I set my cup down and began to pull out brushes, rollers, and wood stain so I could work on some signposts we were making for one of the campuses of a large corporation. Sometimes I think best when my hands are busy. I positioned the paint tray and poured in the dark espresso-colored stain.

Flash watched my every move with inquisitive eyes, then stepped forward to inspect the color in the tray. With his nose just above the stain, he seemed to give me the okay to proceed. If only hooves had thumbs! (We take being able to give a "thumbs-up" so for granted, don't we? Imagine how hard it would be to function with hooves for hands. And texting? Impossible.)

Flash approved the stack of four-by-four posts that were awaiting stain and assembly, but found fault with the rope that had tied them together, which was now carelessly tossed aside. He picked it up with his teeth and shook it vigorously in front of me. He was right: Ropes shouldn't be left around, waiting for someone to trip on them. Chastened, I took the rope from his mouth, looped it around my arm, and hung it on a nail.

Post after post. It felt like the job of staining them took forever. But Flash hung in there, keeping me company and offering silent suggestions. A tail swish here, an ear twitch there. He guzzled the last sip of my coffee, then stepped on the Styrofoam cup when he was through. He bit off a chunk of the cup and let it dangle from his lips in comic relief. I can't say he was a whole lot of help with my project, but I began to see something about him that made me understand this idea of serving.

Tom's joking comment was all wrong: Flash wasn't completely worthless.

He was just serving in other ways.

Flash was serving up some of the best sermons I'd ever heard . . . all without saying a single word.

Those biblical donkeys. Meghan and her friends. Chris Kyle.

Ordinary characters from ordinary towns, whose service to others made them extraordinary. Humble ones who had found what they were made to do. They served in obscurity, looked for no personal glory, and simply gave of themselves.

They walked.

They did what was asked.

They did what donkeys and people do best: They served.

In the process of serving, they bestowed value on those they served.

And in the act of giving, they changed the world. They became part of God's unfolding, amazing grace.

I realized that God takes regular people— unassuming individuals who are willing to play supporting roles—and uses them in His grand story that's being played out on eternity's stage. He takes those who are willing to be saddled up, loaded down, and given the task of serving, and He puts them in places where their abilities can best be used.

Maybe you're not asked to do something noteworthy or remarkable. Maybe you are simply called to walk alongside someone for eighty miles. To be a friend to someone who needs a friend. Or to do that one kind thing that no one will ever know you did. Maybe it's washing a needy woman's laundry. Maybe it's helping her shower. Maybe it's arranging flowers at a small funeral in a tiny chapel. Maybe it's working at a post overseas, away from family and friends, for months on end. Maybe it's changing diapers, washing dishes, helping with homework, being a scout leader, or mowing an elderly neighbor's yard.

This is what we are made for.

To serve.

To love.

To give.

And I could see it so clearly.

Being part of His grace story means allowing your life to be bookended by two donkey rides. You enter and you exit, in humble service. It means that you are defined by what you give, not by what you have. Your life is marked not by talent, but by commitment. Not by beauty, but by sturdy hooves and a willing heart.

"Be a service animal. You are made to serve in love."

I wrote the words in my journal, my fingers espresso-colored from the project I had just finished. I knew it would take days for the stain to work itself out from under my fingernails. *Oh well.* I turned my hands over and raised my palms up in a silent prayer. Flash stepped forward to see if there was anything edible cupped inside, then looked up at me in inquiry.

"Baby, there's nothing here for you." I shook my head and paused for a moment, wondering if he'd understand. "I'm . . . I'm giving these hands to God right now." Rough and stained, small and empty. But ready to work, willing to give. Flash nuzzled my palms and nodded in agreement, his brown eyes upon me and soft ears pricked forward. He blinked his dark lashes, and I put my arms around his neck.

This donkey. This service animal. This God who whispered through him.

"Let me serve others in love, the way I was made to do." My prayer floated past the corrugated metal roof and gnarled tree branches and into the winter sky above.

Be a service animal.
You are made to serve in love.

CHAPTER 10

Change Comes Calling

There was change in the wind. Not nickels and dimes floating through the air, because imagine how much it would hurt if you got pelted by random coins.

No, the type of change that blew in was different. It felt like a chilly March morning, all gray and damp, when you're outside in your jacket with your fingers tucked into your sleeves and shoulders hunched with chin down against the wind. And out of nowhere, there is a flicker of dappled sunlight that falls on your furrowed forehead, and it feels warm for a tiny moment before skittering away. *Did I really feel that? Or did I imagine it? No, those clouds are too heavy for the sun to break through.*

But then, a bit later, you feel that sun on your face again, this time for a couple of seconds, just long enough for you to uncurl your fingers to try to catch it before it's gone. It, too, darts away, but you *know* you felt it. You had to squint in the brightness, and now there is a funny pattern on the insides of your eyelids from the unexpected shaft of light. And even though the rest of the day is still gray and damp and chilly, you feel a tiny bit hopeful and happy inside because you experienced those two fleeting moments (well, maybe just one because the first one could have been your imagination).

Suddenly you think about Easter eggs and the fact that you haven't used up all the firewood and haven't worn your cute boots enough this winter. You realize you should have put tulip bulbs in the refrigerator *weeks* ago, and it's already too late if you want to have blooms this year. The Christmas wreath that somehow never got packed up with the rest of the holiday decor (you were okay with leaving it out because it seemed "wintery" and not too "Christmasy," and you also didn't feel like climbing into the attic to put it away) now seems horribly out of place. *Spring is upon us. We can't have a fake pine wreath on the door!*

You think about all this, even though it's just as cold and miserable out as it was ten minutes ago. You couldn't wait for a hint of sunshine and a break in the clouds to signal a new season, but now that it's here, you realize you aren't even close to being ready for it.

That's what one waft of change (maybe two, depending on how you count them) can do.

^ ^

I stood at the kitchen window and watched Grayson hit golf balls into the field just beyond the front yard. He lined up his driver, shifting weight between feet and taking a couple of short swings to center the ball on his club. His tongue worked his lower lip in concentration. His arms swung the club back in classic golf form. *Whack!* The ball flew out over the tall grass and into the oaks along the dry creek bed.

Beau, who once loved retrieving balls, sat in quiet repose nearby, content with being an armchair athlete these days. His hips and declining eyesight kept him sidelined, but he never complained. Both Gray and Beau were getting older, but only one of them was getting bigger and stronger with each year. The other took to napping and tail wagging as forms of exercise. Grayson reached down and tried to talk Beau into fetching, but he wasn't too keen on leaving his comfy spot on the grass to futilely search for a ball in the thicket.

"I think I'm going to set up a practice area for Gray in the barn." Tom's voice drifted over my shoulder as he came up behind me to see what was happening. "He's really motivated to get good at it, and he wants to practice his swing as much as he can. But he's losing so many balls in the field out there, and it's frustrating trying to find them." He scratched his chin. "I've got some netting that we could hang across the opening. Then all we'd really need to do is make a little tee-off area, and we'd be set."

This sounded simple enough, so the boys went to work. Of course, Flash was on hand to oversee the project. No telling how they would have messed it up otherwise. He watched as they raised the netting into place and secured it on the top and sides. Half of the three-sided barn was open but covered by the tin roof; this would allow Grayson to stand inside, out of the elements, to practice.

Flash had little to say about the proceedings, although we noted his agitation when the teeing green was placed in the center of the open area. A piece of plywood covered with artificial turf, it would make a good place for Grayson to work on his swing. Flash sniffed the surface and nibbled at the corner with his teeth.

"Flash, that's not real grass, you silly." We chuckled at him and then became slightly puzzled when his front hoof came down on it with a thud. He blew hard through his nostrils and stamped once again.

"Hey, buddy," Tom soothed him. He moved close to Flash and ran his hand along his back, then leaned on his shoulders to get him to step back. Tom looked him in the eye. "You're not telling me you're objecting to the golf stuff in here, are you?"

Flash shook his ears as if to show his indifference and then turned on his heel and moseyed out. I guess he was just having some fun with us.

Anxious to try out his new practice area, Grayson awoke early the next morning to get a few swings in before school. How handy to have everything all set up! He hurried out to the barn.

Minutes later he was back, a strange look on his face. "Mom, the barn has been vandalized! You need to come and see this."

I followed him outside and stopped in my tracks at the sight.

The turf-covered plywood tee had been destroyed. It was dragged off to the side, dented and covered with dirt. In its place, someone had cleared the layers of loose dirt and wood shavings, exposing the hard ground. The netting had been torn on one side and was hanging limply from the upper beam. An overturned chair lay in the corner. It looked as if a tornado had blown through.

But the *coup de grâce* was right in front of us. It was a pile of donkey poop, smack in the middle of the dirt floor.

A calling card, if you will.

This was the work of one angry donkey.

It suddenly came to me. *Oh my. Just like the Christmas boxes.* How could we have forgotten? A few years earlier, after the holidays, I had packed up the decorations and put the boxes in the barn's open area for temporary storage. Flash had waited until he thought no one was looking before attacking the boxes. We heard the sound of cardboard breaking and the tinkling of ornaments being smashed before we realized what was happening. *Good-bye, 1989 Hallmark Snoopy ornament and untold number of lights.*

And then there was the Workbench Fiasco. How quickly it

had been erased from our memories. But now that you mention it, who *could* forget the mayhem that ensued when a worktable was introduced to the stall area before the barn renovation took place? The stall was unused. Flash's name was not over the door. Nobody had claim to it. It was a perfectly logical place to set up shop for the various projects we had going on.

That is, logical to everyone *except* a certain long-eared, opinionated member of the equine family, who shall go unnamed. The table was at the perfect height for a large, fuzzy muzzle to sniff and inspect everything. One easy swipe of the nose, and it could all be overturned and knocked to the ground. The tools, the wood, the papers, the measuring tape, the work gloves. In and out, a smooth operation by an experienced vandal.

And how is it that we did not consider the New Fence Situation? Tom tried repeatedly to run a new fence around a small section of the pasture in which he had created a hockey training area for the teams he coached. He made stations out of synthetic ice that had been donated to him so the players could practice shooting pucks in what is called "dryland training." He did not need a six-hundred-pound donkey walking across the synthetic ice or pooping in inconvenient locations. Or moving the synthetic ice sheets or nibbling at the targets. But somehow Flash managed to sneak through the barricades and magically appear out of nowhere in the cordoned-off area. He'd nonchalantly graze, as if nothing were out of the ordinary. If he couldn't stop the change from happening, at least he could pretend it didn't affect him.

Then there was the Utility Trailer Incident, which we won't go into here, except to quietly mention that Flash didn't appreciate having it parked near his favorite roll spot in the pasture. And also that he "unloaded" (which, in this instance, means "forcibly removed by means of chomping into, dragging, and dumping out") the contents of the trailer to get to the bag of feed at the bottom.

It's safe to say that Flash welcomes change, just as long as nothing is different or altered in any way.

"Too much change for one day." Hands in pockets, Tom assessed the golf carnage and delivered his pronouncement. "We should have done this gradually." He pulled the tattered tee platform from beneath the dirt to mend it and stapled the net back in place. I shoveled the "calling card." We would try again.

Next day, same thing. Tee kicked and buried under dirt, net torn down, roll spot cleared, chair overturned, poop pile front and center. At least Flash was consistent. And, apparently, *regular*. Oddly, he always looked just as surprised as everyone else each morning when we came in to inspect the damage.

"Don't look at me," he shrugged with a *phhhht*, his lips vibrating like a motorboat. As if there could be anyone else. There was no remorse. Only a slight twitch of his large ears that belied his smug claim of innocence.

We continued in this pattern on and off for days until the destruction gradually ceased. Flash never really liked the golf equipment in there, but after a while he was content with merely kicking dirt over the tee and walking over it whenever he felt like it to show his disdain for the changes. He wanted everything to stay exactly as it had been, with himself in control of his little world.

And I couldn't blame him. I felt the same way.

Because things were shifting in my little world outside the barn. Somehow, Grayson grew taller than me, and I wasn't sure when that had happened, exactly. His feet hung off the end of his bed at night, and when I tucked him in, I noticed how his frame now filled the full-size mattress. He would be heading off to college soon, and there were applications to fill out, tests to take, and lots of new things to experience. I was excited for him but suddenly felt uncertain about who I'd be without children under my care. My chest was heavy and light at the same time.

Lauren and Robert were hoping to start a family soon, and my head nearly exploded at the thought. It was just a few years ago that I had grieved over the loss of Collin and desperately wanted to fill the vacancy in my heart with a new baby, and now . . . now my oldest child was thinking of having babies of her own.

Meghan, grown and married, was teaching elementary music. Such happy, wonderful changes, but if I'd had a box to stomp on or a chair to overturn, I might have done it.

A shaft of sunlight on a furrowed brow. Fingers clenched in sleeves, refusing to unfurl.

∧ ∧

An e-mail landed in my in-box. It was from a complete stranger, asking if I would be interested in speaking at her church's women's retreat in Illinois.

"I've been reading your blog, and your words have touched me. I wonder if you might come and share with my ladies this fall," she wrote. I reread it several times to make sure I understood the request. Because I wanted to be certain that the terror I felt was well grounded.

Run with horses, Rachel. Run with horses. Or just run.

So, of course, I immediately put the e-mail aside. I formulated my gracious decline. "Thank you for your lovely invitation, but I am currently paralyzed from the eyes down, and I'm also busy that weekend, and every other weekend, with a thing."

I could never stand up and speak to a group of women. Remember the drooling and the blacking out in the business meeting? I'm still not over it. Plus, I have nothing to say. Blogging is one thing, namely baring your soul to the world from behind a computer screen. I'd been writing online for years, something I'd come to love as a creative outlet and as a way to help others find a sense of sanctuary in their busy lives. I had no problem with that. Speaking is another thing, namely sharing your expertise with people who are actually *present* in the room, staring back at you and taking notes. I'm pretty much terrified of that.

The familiar voices began whispering: You're a failure. A fraud. You don't have anything to share out loud. You're too unworthy. You're not good enough.

Remember your name. Remember whose you are. Wait. What's your name again?

"I would like to talk more with you about your event," I typed back. Not exactly a no, but also not a yes. A noncommittal reply might buy me some time. Perhaps the lady would go away.

"When may I call you?" came the response. She wasn't going away.

"Tuesday at 10:00 a.m. would work great!" Why I was using an exclamation point was beyond me. What I really wanted to do was run and hide.

Find your refuge in Me. You can hide in the shelter of My wings.

As we began having phone conversations about the event, I found myself turning to the pages of my journals and blog posts and sorting through old, scribbled notes. Even as the ground beneath my feet felt shaky, I started to see some messages within the scribbles. A phrase here, a Scripture there, a donkey story in a margin of a notebook.

Say yes, Rachel. Don't let fear keep you from moving forward. Keep putting one foot in front of the other. Blaze a new trail.

A date was set and airline tickets purchased. I committed to it, and there could be no turning back. But there was still regular work to be done. Ladders to haul, sketches to draw, projects to complete, bills to pay, dinners to make. The clouds above were still heavy, but I knew I'd felt a ray of warmth on my face that made me think a new season might be ahead. *Or did I imagine it?*

The retreat went well, I thought. I had prepared like crazy for my speaking sessions and obsessed over my hair. Obviously, the timing of root touch-ups is crucial. You cannot afford to underplan this. And because my hair looked so good, I hoped it made up for what I lacked in smooth sentence transitions. I returned home with a pocket full of sweet thank-you notes and a little taste of confidence. Wow!

And there were bigger opportunities. Some months later, I found myself sitting across the table from a top talent manager in Nashville. I'd been invited there to discuss representation and to explore the prospects of starting a speaking tour, marketing my art, and writing a book. *Me.* Seriously? My head spun with ideas and possibilities! What an incredible turn of events.

But this time, I totally botched it. I didn't return phone calls, missed a deadline, and avoided making the commitment. In short, I choked. "This won't work if I want it for you more than you want it for you," the talent manager told me. And I knew she was right.

It's funny how you yearn for change, for something new, for a lucky chance, for an end to the monotony, for life as you know it to just stop, to just go away . . . and then when that change comes, you start backpedaling and pulling out every reason you want things to stay the same. You think of all the ways you're not ready. You think of all the things you'll miss. You even do things to sabotage moving forward.

I remember as a kid sitting in the "way back" seat of the family station wagon, a car that was roughly the length of an ocean liner, with faux wood paneling on the sides. We loved the fact that it had automatic windows and was the perfect shade of avocado green.

The "way back" seat was the one that got pulled up from the storage area in the rear and faced backward. I can still feel the sensation of barreling toward a destination I could not see while watching through the back window as the road fell away behind us. The dashed lane markers seemed to emerge from somewhere below, all huge and oversized, then quickly get smaller and smaller until they disappeared as tiny dots into nothingness. It felt like time travel, but with motion sickness. Everyone knows it's a terrible idea to ride in a vehicle backward. Don't even *think* about reading a book, unless you have a barf bag handy.

But moving toward a destination you can't see? Watching the past, where you've been, fall away? Even as new seasons of opportunities and personal growth were around the bend, I wanted to hold on to everything I had, everything I'd known. This life—this beautiful, messy life—was changing once again, and there was so much I hadn't done in *this* season yet.

Grayson's last years at home felt bittersweet. When we'd moved to this funky barn house, he was eight. *Eight!* A kid with an orthodontic appliance and a penchant for building model airplanes. Lauren and Meghan were in high school and fixated on their hair (I don't know where they got that), choir, youth group, and a dizzying schedule of activities. Flash arrived just as they were leaving, and I came to believe he was a little gift from above to occupy my mind and assuage the mama-ache.

Now the girls had made it all the way through college and into new marriages, and Grayson was heading off to study aerospace engineering . . . and I couldn't be more proud. Or more brokenhearted.

How many times had I wished I could walk down the driveway, away from motherhood and work projects and all the laundry? How many tense discussions had Tom and I had over household rules, chores, activities, haircuts, and homework that made me want to run away? How often had I complained about the Explorer and the workload and the burden of shaping young lives, which always felt more like herding cats than actual shaping?

Now, motherhood was falling away behind me, and I was hurtling toward a destination I couldn't see. A great unknown. I wasn't prepared for parenthood to disappear as a tiny dot into nothingness. I hadn't even started their scrapbooks yet! And I had forgotten to show Grayson how to fold fitted sheets. My earlier confidence that I would accomplish these things before the kids left now made me feel awfully presumptuous.

And to top it all off, the horses next door disappeared. Flash's baby mama, his darling little mule, and the rest of the group just up and moved off with their owner somewhere. *No!* I leaned on the gate, still wired shut from the night Flash had broken the hinge, and scanned the field for any trace of them. Nothing. It felt strange and empty, like one more thing had slipped through my grasp.

The gate protested my weight with a squeak, as if telling me to move on. But one look at Flash's expression told me that moving on wouldn't be so easy. They'd been such ideal companions for him, hanging their heads over the fence and shooting the breeze with him each day. Now who would Flash have?

Certainly not Beau, the object of his unaffection. Something would have to be done, but I didn't want to consider that now.

A puff of wind, change in the air. A phone call to come and speak. An invitation to write for a high-profile blog. A botched chance at stardom. An opportunity for our business to change. Kids driving off with a trunk full of belongings. A month in which projects took place in front of a computer screen instead of on a ladder with a paintbrush in hand.

Still juggling, still keeping as many balls in the air as you can, because you never know when you'll need one of them. You think you have an idea how everything is going to turn out, and in a moment of clarity find out you're riding backward and someone else is driving the station wagon. You fight for control. Stomp a box. Leave a calling card.

And in the end, you let go.

Suddenly, all the lessons I had learned from Flash came flooding in. Refuge, remembering your name, running with horses, wearing your donkey heart on your sleeve, finding your passion, serving others. . . .

All along, God had been quietly teaching me through a charming, bucktoothed, opinionated, sweet donkey. And now He was guiding me—*us*—through more changes. Would I keep kicking and resist anything altered or different, or would I learn to apply the lessons and adjust my old ways of thinking? Would I open my arms to new experiences, or be so focused on the present and the past that I'd miss them?

My little notes, on scraps of paper here and there, were being challenged to come to life . . . to become *real*. To take on skin and bones, and breathe in air, and become more than cute axioms taped to my desk. If God was real and true, and deeply involved with the details of my life, then all of this was for *something*. Nothing would be wasted.

But only if I chose to embrace a new season.

Flash figured out that throwing a temper tantrum and destroying the things he could not change were futile attempts to control his little world. Once he realized that there was nothing to fear, and that good things could come from the changes he resisted, he settled down. He learned that the changes, like the golf and hockey areas and the workshop, brought *people* into his world. And more people equaled more attention. More attention equaled a happy donkey. He just couldn't see it at the time. Oddly, getting his ears scratched more often helped him come around to this deep spiritual truth: Change is a good thing.

Much of the time, the changes we face feel like little more than nearly imperceptible puffs of wind. C. S. Lewis once said, "Isn't it funny how day by day nothing changes, but when you look back, everything is different." The incremental shifts, the tiny tectonic movements, the way your kid's face loses that baby softness and becomes lean and chiseled, without your even noticing until you watch him sleep one night. The way you give everything you have to life and think it's nothing much to offer, but there it is. *Take it.* And the way it starts coming back to you.

The patterns on the insides of your eyelids tell you the sun has poked through the clouds, for just a moment, and there is change in the air.

You must unfurl your fingers to catch the first rays.

Embrace change.
Don't let fear of the unknown keep you from moving forward.

CHAPTER 11
Beau

Sorry about Beau." Grayson shrugged apologetically and motioned with his head to the dripping yellow Lab. I slid the glass door open to greet them in the breezeway, and a muggy blast of summer air pushed its way in as I stepped outside. Beau planted his feet, shaking pond water from his body in a violent vibration that started at his nose and ended at the tip of his thick tail. He sneezed and looked up at me with an expression of sheer joy.

"I had him in the boat with me, but he jumped into the water to cool off and then went for a swim," Gray explained, setting his tackle box down and untying his muddy shoes. "You know how he is."

"Oh brother. Beau, you're going to smell for two days." I chided the dog, but he didn't seem the least bit concerned with my scolding. He lumbered to his water dish and lapped at it noisily before flopping down on the cool cement floor. He sounded like a sponge hitting pavement, the water splattering outward from his saturated fur coat.

He's going to be stiff for days, too, I thought. Dear old Beau. But maybe the swim was good for his arthritis. I was happy that he had enjoyed some physical activity—something he'd always loved as a younger dog.

For years, Beau's powerful physique made him the perfect country companion: He regularly raced the Explorer up the driveway, clocking an easy twenty miles per hour on the quarter-mile run to the house. He loped along by the right front tire, pink tongue flapping from the side of his mouth, until the sound of the gas being applied caused him to engage his afterburners. Head tucked and tongue retracted, his mighty front paws pulled the earth beneath him, and his muscular hind legs propelled him forward in a golden blur. The race always ended in a tie, Beau braking to wag his entire body in excited welcome.

The dog could keep fetching sticks tossed into the pond long after your arm could possibly continue throwing. He'd leap into the water with a giant *ka-ploosh*, swim out to the stick, pick it up with his teeth, and circle back around toward shore. Sometimes he'd just paddle around the pond with the stick, as if he was so happy to be fetching that he didn't know what to do with himself except take a couple of extra laps. If you depleted your supply of sticks (or if your arm gave out, whichever came first), he'd grab a giant log floating in the water and bring it to you. His love of water also made him a natural hunting dog. He could sit motionless in a duck blind for hours, then swim through icy water to retrieve fallen birds.

Beau took it upon himself to guard the entire property with his daily circuits along the fence lines, his nose and tail working from side to side, and making use of his bottomless bladder by marking his territory with boundless enthusiasm. He chased off wandering dogs and coyotes, scared up birds, and sent bunnies scurrying into their holes; but then he would come back and graciously allow the girls' kittens to pounce all over him and play with his tail.

Beau, one hundred pounds of friendly, covered in nearly white, shedding fur, had once been an "outside only" dog, and I liked it that way. But somehow, he had finagled his way indoors during the coldest nights of winter and the hottest days of summer . . . and gradually, everything in between. His wet black nose and pleading brown eyes were difficult to resist, and since he was good about staying off the carpeted areas of the house, we allowed him in.

Well, I take that back. He wasn't *that* good about staying off the carpeted areas. He was very good about *staying downstairs*—on the carpet, of course. And he was only good about the downstairs part until one October night, about a year after we'd moved in.

∧ ∧

"Tommy, wake up!" I shook Tom awake at the sound of a peculiar noise coming from the other room. Something, or someone, was moving around Grayson's bedroom in the middle of the night. My hands clutched Tom's arm. An intruder? A burglar?

We held our breath and listened a moment longer, our heartbeats pounding in our ears. Tom slowly slid out of bed and crept to the door. He stepped through the small hallway at the top of the stairs and paused at Grayson's door to peer inside. I heard him let out his breath.

"Rachel, it's okay," he whispered. "Come in here." I flipped the covers back to follow him.

The moonlight filtered through Grayson's window blinds, revealing the silhouette of our intruder, who was standing next to the bed of our then nine-year-old son. It was Beau. With his nose just inches from Grayson's face, he watched the boy breathe, his chest rising and falling. In. Out. In. Out. The tip of the dog's tail moved slightly, letting us know that he was aware of our presence, but his resolute profile didn't waver an inch.

"What's going on, Beau?" He'd never challenged our downstairs-only rule before. Tom patted the dog's head and reached forward to straighten Grayson's pillow. He turned to me in alarm.

"Gray's burning up," Tom said, feeling his forehead and pulling off the blankets. I ran to get cool washcloths and medicine to bring his fever down.

The next morning, a trip to the doctor's office and X-rays at the hospital revealed pneumonia in Grayson's lungs. We'd known that Grayson didn't feel well when we put him to bed that night, but we had no idea how serious his illness was. Yet somehow, Beau sensed it. For the next three nights, the dog remained at his bedside until the antibiotics began to work and the worst was over. His buddy needed him.

I guess we figured Beau had earned the right to go upstairs and sleep wherever he wanted. Mostly, he chose to curl up on the small hooked rug next to Grayson's bed, right where the boy's hand could reach down and scratch his blocky head, causing the dog's heavy tail to thump on the floor at odd hours of the night.

∧ ∧

I looked at Beau now, soggy and happy from his afternoon swim. "Walk with me to the barn," I called to him. "It will help you dry off and keep you from stiffening up." He pulled himself up, his hind legs reluctant, and gave another vigorous shake before accompanying me to the gate.

Lifting the heavy chain from the nail, I pushed the metal gate open and stepped into the pasture. The ground was hard and dry under my feet, and the sparse summer grass clung to the cracked earth for dear life. Beau stopped at the fence post and sat down, refusing to go any farther. He was at The Line.

The Line had been drawn from day one of Flash's residency, and it followed the fence exactly. The pie-shaped pasture on one side of the fence was Flash's territory, with the remaining land on the other side belonging to Beau. Made of wood posts connected by galvanized wire mesh, the fence provided the legal framework for the two animals to work within. Beau was respecting his limits.

"You stay on your side, and I'll stay on mine" were the general terms of agreement the two abided by. But there were exceptions, such as these laid out by Flash:

1. Dog may enter pasture when accompanied by a human.
2. Dog may not drink from donkey's water bucket.
3. Dog may sit in barn, but only if accompanied by humans.
4. Dog may not bark, whine, or look appealing while donkey completes his interaction with said humans.
5. Dog is not permitted to make eye contact with donkey.

Beau, for his part, had his own stipulations:

1. Donkey may not bray in dog's presence.
2. Donkey must be on a lead at all times when outside pasture territory.
3. Donkey may not kick or bite, but may sniff and stand quietly in dog's presence.
4. Donkey may graze in the yard, under strict supervision by humans, and only when tied to a stake.

5. Donkey may make eye contact with dog, on a limited basis.

6. Donkey may not eat dog food. (To my knowledge, this was never an actual issue, but Beau felt strongly about his food, so . . . you know.)

"Oh, come on, boy." I reasoned with him at The Line. "I'll be right with you the whole time. It's okay." At my reassurance, Beau resumed his walk to the barn and sniffed out a perfect spot to sit and watch the evening proceedings. Tom was already there, cleaning out Flash's stall and putting a flake of fresh hay in the feeding rack.

"So what's the deal with these two, anyway?" Tom asked as he set a new bag of wood shavings on the ground. I picked up a rake that leaned against the plywood wall and watched as Flash sauntered in to check out our activity.

"I don't know. I don't get it," I said, setting the rake aside and rubbing Flash's forehead.

Clumps of dirt and blades of dried grass clung to his coat from his last dust roll, giving him a rugged, tousled appearance. As much as he likes being brushed and fussed over, I must say he wears the rough outdoorsman look best.

With a nod of his head, the donkey dismissed Beau from his vantage point in the corner and then positioned himself directly in front of me. The yellow Lab, his head low and eyes averted according to code, made a wide circle past Flash and took a seat under the shade of a mesquite tree just beyond the barn. He gave a resigned yawn and lowered himself to the ground, settling his head on his front legs. Satisfied that the dog was out of range, Flash swished his tail and inquired about a treat.

I pulled a few burrs from his mane and then stepped toward the tack room to grab a small cookie from a jar just inside the door. Animal crackers—Flash's favorite. He eagerly poked his head in, blocking my exit as his mouth moved in anticipation.

"Back up, Flash," I said. "You need to be a gentleman." I waited until he stepped backward, then opened my palm with the treat inside. It was gone in an instant, Flash's deft top lip picking up the cookie in a swift movement. He was already looking for more before he even swallowed it. I acquiesced with a second cookie. Okay, a third one too. *But that's all. I mean it. Really, I do. No more, Flash.*

"I think they got off to a rocky start and never really recovered," I said, turning to Tom, who was now dumping the shavings into the stall. "Beau is still bent out of shape over Flash trying to kick him that first day."

"That's a long time to hold a grudge," Tom replied thoughtfully. "I find it hard to believe they aren't the best of friends by now. I mean, there's absolutely no reason they can't get along. They're both friendly, loyal, sweet, and lovable." He counted their attributes off with his fingers.

"Right," I laughed, "just not to each other!" I looked at the dog, nearly dry in the late afternoon heat. "I wonder if Beau feels resentful about Flash taking over the pasture. I think he wishes he had this area back in his control."

"Well, Beau does take his guard duties very seriously. Remember how he used to walk the perimeter of the entire property each day? He never includes the pasture anymore. He leaves that part up to Flash to take care of. Maybe he feels Flash isn't doing a good enough job."

"You'd think he'd be grateful to the donkey for taking it off his hands, er . . . paws . . . whatever. With Beau's hips bothering him these days, he can barely get all the way around his own area, let alone the pasture. It's taking him longer and longer to complete his rounds, poor guy."

I pulled the rake across the clean stall material to even it out. There isn't a better smell than wood chips and hay, mingled with manure, cedar, and sweet feed.

"Flash hasn't helped the situation, though," Tom said wryly. He crumpled the bag of wood shavings and moved over to the donkey. "Most of the time, he treats Beau like he barely exists. I mean, he's happy to let the dog hang out at a distance, and he doesn't seem to care that we pay attention to him. But you never really see him act friendly with him, either. There's definitely a wall there."

"It's like they're indifferent toward each other," I concluded. "I think they decided early on that they would coexist and cooperate, like how they tag-team our walks, yet not become emotionally involved with each other."

Tom cocked an eyebrow. "Emotionally involved? Right, Dr. Phil. I don't know how 'emotionally involved' a donkey can be." Just then Flash rubbed his ears on Tom's arm and gave him a soulful look. Tom wrapped Flash's neck in a hug, his cheek resting on the knob of his head.

"Uh-huh. Well, he's certainly emotionally involved with *you*," I observed. "Look at him. He loves you!"

"What, this? Nah, this is just us messing around." He gave Flash a playful push to prove it. Flash returned the affection by leaning back into him, knocking Tom off balance and garnering a snicker out of me. I could have sworn Flash smiled.

From his isolation spot, Beau whined in jealousy. He loved

nothing better than a bit of roughhousing, and it hurt his feelings not to be invited to play.

"What a shame. Beau is such a great dog, and Flash is a perfect donkey. Think of all they're missing! Do you think there is any hope for friendship between them?"

Beau struggled to his feet, and I could see he was already stiff from overdoing it in the pond. His right back leg didn't want to cooperate with his forward motion, and it sort of hung suspended for the first few steps back to the house. Although he'd never admit it, roughhousing would have been out of the question anyway.

That night, Beau made it only halfway up the steps to Grayson's room. The landing would have to do for now, and he lowered himself down with a groan. Back end collapsing, front end following suit. Black nose on giant paws. The faint aroma of *eau de pond*.

I wish now that Last Times would come with big signs that say, "This is the Last Time." Then you would know that you should savor them, no matter how inconsequential they are. Like the last time you put sugar in your tea before you swore off sweets, or the last time you used a push mower, or the last time you tucked extra underwear in your kid's backpack, just in case. You might have stopped to just feel the moment, breathe it in, and let it get fixed in your memory like a Polaroid photograph.

The last time you rocked your baby to sleep. The last time you stepped on a Lego piece in the middle of the night. The last time you tasted your grandmother's rhubarb pie. The last time you kissed your father good night. If you had known it was the last time, you would have closed your eyes and said to yourself, *I must remember this. I must remember the smell of this kitchen and this coffee and this pie. I must remember this scratchy flannel shirt and this smell of Old Spice. I must remember the feel of this downy head on my shoulder, and this milky breath and these tiny fingers curled around a blankie.*

You'd say, *I must remember this dog, and how he slept on a hooked rug next to a boy's bed.*

Instead, you rush on. You think there will be a hundred other times, exactly like this one, and you look at your watch or mutter some annoyance or answer the phone or become distracted in some way. You don't fix it in your mind, you don't stop, and you don't *feel* it. Because why should you when there will be other chances, and life is so busy, and there are so many things to do? You'll savor it next time, or maybe the time after that one. You didn't realize at the moment that this—*this* would be the last time. It wouldn't be coming around again. And you missed it.

I missed it.

∧ ∧

That's how I felt about the last time Beau curled up next to Grayson's bed. It had come and gone without me even realizing it. Gray was almost grown-up, and it seemed like the lamp on his nightstand was always on much later than mine as he worked on calculus equations and physics problems for the next day's homework assignment. "What time do you need to get up in the morning?" I'd ask, already thinking about tomorrow's tasks as I kissed his head and picked up socks from the floor.

When the landing on the stairs became the new place Beau liked to sleep, I figured it was because he received a pat on the head from every person who passed by. I didn't really stop to think that he'd never make it to the second floor again and into the boy's room for another night. Or that soon, he'd only make it to the rug by the fireplace because climbing to the landing halfway up the stairs would be too much work for those arthritis-ridden legs.

When the day came where Beau went outside and surveyed the property from the edge of the yard instead of walking the fence line and marking his whole territory, I never really imagined he had permanently retired from his sentinel duties. Lately, he simply watched the Explorer make its way up the driveway, choosing to greet us at the door rather than meet us on the road and race us home. I guess I missed the last run, too.

"Hey, Old Guy," we called him. Beau was hard of hearing and not able to see well, but his tail still worked beautifully— *thump, thump, thump.* Sensing a simple turn of the head in his direction, he'd start thumping his tail in anticipation of attention. By now, we were regularly hosing him off outside. The smell was exactly what you'd expect from an incontinent dog—and that's when all the Last Times began to dawn on us.

"Hey, Old Guy, let's go get the mail," I said, looking for a reason to get him up from his bed in the kitchen. "It will be good for you to get a little exercise." It took a while to convince him to leave his soft cushion, but he managed to make his way to the door and over the threshold. Immediately I could see that a half-mile round-trip walk to the mailbox would be too much.

"On second thought, let's just check on Flash's water instead." We switched course and turned toward the gate. Flash was at his salt block, which sits in the shade of the cedar trees that line the fence. His tongue methodically worked over the red-colored brick of minerals, his eyes half-closed as he licked.

At the sound of our feet, he looked up and immediately made his way toward us. He met Beau and me at the fence post, where the dog tucked his tail and sat sideways on his best leg.

The passage of time seemed to be softening the donkey's attitude as well as his rules. As I paused to lift the chain, he lowered his oversize head to Beau's level. Flash's big brown eyes rested on the dog's soft eyes, now cloudy with age, and they held each other's gaze for a long moment. The donkey's nostrils opened wide as he gently sniffed at the dog, who brought his nose up to the white muzzle that reached across the divide. Four hooves on one side of The Line, four paws on the other. Two sets of ears pricked forward. Two noses, meeting in the middle.

"Well, how about that?" I whispered. Wonders never cease. I eased the gate open to step inside, then nudged Flash over so I could open it wide enough for the dog to go through. Beau hesitated, then crossed The Line and turned to the donkey, tail slowly wagging. Flash gave him an amiable nod, ears turning, eyes welcoming, and together the three of us headed to the water bucket—at the halting pace of a gimpy Lab. A thaw had begun.

For as often as you wish you could know when something is the Last Time, you'll find a way to pretend that a Real Last Time isn't one. Years earlier, when I'd said good-bye to my grandfather, who was in a wheelchair and suffering from Alzheimer's disease, I pretended that I'd be back to the nursing home real soon. *It isn't the last time,* I said to myself. *I'll be back and we'll talk about baseball, and he'll show me some moves he learned as a catcher, and we will plan to make lutefisk and lefse, his favorite Norwegian delights.*

When we locked the door to our house in the city for the

last time, we acted as if we were going on vacation. "Did we turn off the water? Check to see that the lights were off? Is the back gate closed? Now, let's go have some fun on the beach, or in the mountains." We tried not to look in the rearview mirror as we left the neighborhood where our kids had spent their early childhood years. "We'll take lots of pictures while we're away," we said, "and then we'll return and pick up right where we left off. Everybody buckled in?"

When each of the kids drove off to college, down the driveway in a cloud of dust, we tried to pretend they were just going to the store, maybe to get some milk or a loaf of bread. *They'll be right back,* we told ourselves, swallowing the lumps in our throats and fighting back tears. *Silly to cry over a trip to the store. Just busy yourself in the kitchen or something, and they'll be back in a minute.*

Oh, who are we kidding?

This is the last time, and things will never be the same. It's the truth. I fumble for a tissue and blow my nose. The tears fall, and my bones feel like mush. My head hurts. I hate facing the reality that something precious is gone.

^ ^

I didn't think I was the type to grieve over a dog. After all, I was the one who complained about all the dog hair and all the dirt those paws brought in. The nose prints on the glass door annoyed me. I was so tired of cleaning up after him. And then there were the big blue pads, lined with plastic on one side, absorbent paper on the other. The leaky, elderly dog made the whole house smell. But I loved that dog, and I loved how he was woven into our family history. I loved that he was always there for us. None of us could imagine life without him, and here I was, grieving already.

When the inevitable finally came, Tom dug a grave for the yellow Lab and set white stones all around to mark it. I didn't watch him dig it, and I didn't want to see the fresh mound of earth. I wanted to pretend Beau was down at the pond for an afternoon swim, and that he'd be hungry for dinner and that I'd grouse about him smelling like pond water. But eventually, I made my way to the clearing under the trees to pay my respects and say good-bye. Grayson, Lauren, and Meghan each did the same, on their own time and in their own ways. Tom cried for days, he took it so hard. Mercy, I love that man.

Then it was Flash's turn. We haltered him up and clipped on the lead in silence. He walked readily alongside us, eager for a stroll in the world beyond his pasture. We'd been working on improving his skills on a lead, and we were pleased with his progress. Halfway to Beau's grave, he became engrossed in the grass and took a detour into the yard. Perhaps he wanted to pretend it was just another practice walk, and not a last good-bye. I couldn't blame him; I knew just how he felt. "Come on, buddy. Let's keep going," Tom said, giving a gentle tug on the rope before they continued on together. I followed quietly behind, wanting to give Flash space to take it in.

Flash approached the circle of stones with some reluctance, then brought his head down to smell the new mound. His deep exhale blew the loose soil, and the tiny leaves that had fallen there fluttered up and settled back down. I didn't expect him to say much, and true to form, he didn't. He blinked and turned his ears, then shifted his weight off his back hoof and rested it. From the look of his posture, we would be here awhile. *As it should be.* Tom wiped his cheek with his sleeve as he squatted down next to the donkey's head. Flash understood.

Flash and Beau didn't have a whole lot in common except a love for their people—us. Maybe that was enough. Enough to push them past their petty differences and make them set aside their pride. Maybe they sensed that Last Times were upon them and decided they'd been feuding long enough.

I remembered how Beau had accompanied Flash on guard duty in the pasture that last summer. Flash kept his pace slow for the once-powerful dog who needed to rest every so often before proceeding on. Beau reveled in the morning breezes that blew across the field, his tail wagging and his nose taking in every scent. Flash nibbled on the dry grass as he waited for his friend to mark a new spot or follow a bunny trail. "Take your time," he said with his ears. The donkey never rushed him. Beau repaid his kindness by keeping him company at feeding time and by humoring the occasional brays that once drove him crazy. He remained nearby like an old companion, graciously accepting Flash's opinions and offering a few of his own.

Forgiveness—friendship—had been long in coming, but it arrived just in time. As they held one another's gaze, their eyes said it all:

"I'm sorry I kicked at you."

"I'm sorry I offended you with my exuberance."

"I was wrong to keep you out."

"I never meant to bother you."

"I'm sorry I didn't let you drink from my bucket."

"I'm sorry I drank out of it when you weren't looking. And licked the edge."

It seems like it's always the small stuff that keeps us apart.

The tiny infractions that become larger than life as they fester over time. Lines get drawn. Sides are taken. Heels dig in. "You stay on your side, and I'll stay on mine." "Here are my rules, and don't you dare break them." "This is my territory, and you'd better not enter."

How often do I behave exactly as these two animals had—allowing myself to become offended over some little event . . . getting angry over something insignificant? *Just the tip of the iceberg,* I say inwardly. *Don't give an inch. It's the principle of the thing.*

And on principle, I refuse to forgive. I withhold love. Judge another. Draw that line.

What a shame.

There at Beau's grave, I looked at Flash, with his lower lip drooping and expression sorrowful. His hair was starting to thicken with the approaching autumn season, and it made his face look fuller, fatter. He was lucky that his Last Times with Beau had come with signs. He'd been able to make amends and enjoy their remaining time together. In that moment, I loved Flash more than ever for personifying forgiveness and acceptance and tenderness. And I loved him for mourning the passing of his friend. It went straight to my heart.

Ephesians 4:2 says this: "Always be humble and gentle. Be patient with each other, making allowance for each other's faults because of your love."

We are imperfect creatures, all of us. What a shame to waste our time on trivial differences and self-made rules rather than savoring forgiveness and love and enjoying the richness they bring. We should take someone's hand. We should look our loved ones in the eyes. We should hold a gaze and say the words "I'm sorry" and "I was wrong" and "I forgive you." We should.

We *must*. And we must also say the words "I love you" while we still can. *This* time may be the last chance we'll ever have, but we won't know it until it is gone.

Don't miss it.

Make things right with others.

Don't miss your chance to forgive, accept, and love.

CHAPTER 12

"That's Some Donkey"

MISSING DONKEY.

My heart pounded with anxiety as I typed the words and formatted them in the biggest, boldest font I could fit on a page. The coffee I'd gulped down earlier that day churned in my stomach as I added my phone number and printed off the flyers to staple to telephone poles. I should have eaten a piece of toast, but the thought of food now made me feel sick, given the situation. My hands shook as I gathered the papers from the printer and grabbed my stapler.

Flash was gone.

Oh, where *was* he?

We had no idea. I couldn't believe this had happened. Our donkey was lost. Posting signs to nearby poles was the only thing left I could think of to help us locate Flash and bring him home.

I went over the last twenty-four hours. Weather reports had warned of overnight storms, so we'd spent the evening putting lawn chairs inside, making sure windows were closed, and securing anything we thought might blow away. This is when being married to a true Northerner with a siege mentality is exceptionally advantageous.

I had put some extra hay in Flash's hayrack and given him a good-night pat, but I left the stall door open so he could spend the night wherever he wanted. He still preferred the creek bed in the woods to the noisy metal barn, especially during storms. By now he knew where to stay sheltered, and though I had offered my sensible advice to stay inside the structure, I didn't worry about him.

As promised, the night brought gusty winds and driving rain. Tom and I lay in bed and tried to sleep while we listened to the roof make cracking noises and endured the sounds of branches scraping the windows. "Isn't a fit night out for man nor beast!" Tom quipped in his best Yukon Cornelius voice, and we laughed at the time, feeling happy we'd prepared for it.

Only now it didn't seem so funny. By morning's light, we had found downed branches strewn around the property, trash cans overturned, and worst of all, a pasture gate blown off its hinges into the muddy ground. Uh-oh.

Tom and I clomped through the black clay, which stuck to the bottoms of our boots and added an inch to our overall heights. We put the gate back into place and secured it with rope.

"Hopefully Flash didn't notice the gate down and decide to get out. Any sign of hoofprints?" I asked, peering at the ground around the gate. To our relief, we couldn't see a single one, and we breathed a premature sigh of happiness. *At least Flash is all right*, we thought. Just to be on the safe side, we decided to split up and check the rest of the gates and fences. I headed off toward the barn to set out some morning hay and called for him to come for breakfast.

But no Flash came. I waited. Called again. Waited some more. No donkey.

"Are you sure there weren't any hoofprints?" I queried Tom in the house, then insisted he go back and inspect one more time.

"Nothing, Rachel," Tom assured me. "But that doesn't mean anything. It would be just typical, wouldn't it? Hoofprints are no indication of whether he got out through there or not. Think about how often he materializes on this side of the fence in the hockey area. I don't know how he does it, but somehow he does."

Good point. In addition to the hockey areas, Flash was also

famous for making our rope barricades across the barn open-ings quite irrelevant. Whenever we needed Flash to mind his own business and stay out of our way, we pulled a multilayered, crosshatched system of ropes across the expanse and secured them with a series of eye hooks and carabiners. Too low to the ground to go under, too high to go over, too solid to go through.

That is, for anyone and anything except Flash. He always got through.

But we never actually *saw* him do it. That was the mystery. We could be nearby, engrossed in some barn activity, when sud-denly *there was Flash*. Just nonchalantly scratching some imagi-nary itch with his teeth. Then he'd look up, all like, *Oh hey, what are YOU doing here? I'm just itchy . . . just scratchin' my itch.*

To be honest, it was a little creepy.

Was this disappearance another one of his tricks? We had a full day of work ahead and no time to go chasing down an elusive don-key. I called our client and explained that hopefully this wouldn't take long; we would arrive just a little later than planned to finish her kitchen backsplash. The lady was understanding, although I did have to repeat, "My donkey, yes, that's right, my *donkey* has gone missing. No, not my doggie. My *donkey*, as in *HEE-haw* donkey!" I don't know why that was so hard to understand.

Back outside, Tom and I combed the immediate area. We worked our way from the back of the property, through the yard near the house, and into the woods in front. The problem with—sorry, *one* of the problems with—a brownish-gray don-key is that he blends right into the brush.

We had already learned from experience in the back woods that you could be looking *right at him* and not see him. He loved to make us call him until we were exasperated. All the while, he was silently biding his time from four feet away, still as a statue, and then he'd startle us by moving at full speed. *Whoa, now!* Nostrils flared, with a wild-eyed look, he'd nearly plow us over, barely able to contain his excitement for having pulled a fast one. He'd stop short at the last second, quivering in delight. I've read that donkeys' depth perception is hampered by their wide-set eyes, and I believe it. He always seemed surprised to come upon us so quickly.

We called and whistled. (Well, Tom whistled. I've never gotten the hang of it.) We shook containers of oats.

Nothing. *He'd better not be right under our noses this whole time. I'll kill him.*

We met at the road and then split up again. Tom went east, and I went west along the narrow lane. Calling, whistling (again, not me), and making enticing noises with our buckets. About a half mile down the road, my phone rang. It was Tom.

"This is pointless. He could be anywhere. I think we'd better notify the sheriff's department," Tom said. "That way, if someone reports that they've found him, they'll know to call us." I agreed it was a good approach but secretly hoped our call wouldn't be answered by either of the sheriffs who were around the last time he busted out. I didn't want Flash to be the poster child for "donkey problems." You know how people like to label troublemakers.

But, as fate would have it . . .

"You the donkey people?" It was the deputy from the night of the romantic rendezvous. Sigh. I went ahead and explained our situation. "We'll call you if we hear anything," he said. "Don't worry, we know where you live."

I knew he was writing this on Flash's permanent record, but what choice did we have? We needed his help. By the time I hung up the phone, the coffee I had drunk earlier was making my stomach hurt. Reality started to hit me.

What if Flash never comes back? What if we never find him? What if someone steals him? Could it really be that, in just a few years' time, I'd become so attached to this long-eared character that the thought of losing him now broke my heart? The depth of my emotions caught me off guard. *Don't be silly, Rachel. He's just a donkey.* But I knew he'd become much more than that.

As I gathered up the stack of flyers, the words MISSING DONKEY shouted at me. I momentarily silenced them with prayer.

"God, I know You have much bigger problems to solve today. I know there are wars and famines and people who have serious needs. But would You please help us find Flash? I love him. I believe You gave him to us for a reason. He has been such a blessing. A sweet, crazy blessing. Please bring him home."

I called our client once again and canceled our project for the day, not wanting to be on the opposite side of Dallas if the phone rang. I'm sure she could hear the worry in my voice, and she graciously rescheduled.

As the minutes ticked by, I vaguely remembered an account in the Bible about some missing donkeys. Maybe it would help to read it. After a little digging, I found it in the book of 1 Samuel. I settled in to take my mind off the worry.

Now the donkeys of Kish, Saul's father, were lost.

1 SAMUEL 9:3, ESV

I sat up from my cushioned slouch and did a double take. I could instantly relate. Somehow, I knew this was going to be a good narrative.

Kish, a wealthy man in Israel, instructs his son, Saul, to take a servant and go find a wandering band of donkeys. It probably was not a huge request. The donkeys were likely allowed to graze freely—and, hey, how far can donkeys go, anyway? Pssh. This job just goes along with being a son of a rich guy, and maybe Kish thought a little day trip would be a good experience for him. So Saul and the servant start looking.

They look high and low, up and down and all around, but they cannot find the donkeys anywhere. They keep widening their circle until they've traveled around the entire area. Eventually, their simple task has turned into a three-day, grueling search . . . and still nothing. They've exhausted all of the countryside in their tribe's land and probably are debating whether to scour the neighboring region.

This was sounding familiar.

Saul finally gives up and says to his servant, "We'd better head home. I'm sure my father isn't concerned about the donkeys anymore. But he's probably wondering what happened to us." Somehow, I think Saul may have added a few choice adjectives before the word *donkeys*, but the Scripture writer wisely leaves them out.

The servant has a last-minute, brilliant idea. "Hey! Before we leave, let's go to the next town where a revered prophet lives. Maybe he'll know where the donkeys have wandered to."

Just as they are passing through the gates of the village to find this prophet, who should be coming toward them but the very man they are looking for—Samuel. They are literally about to bump into one another.

It is a holy intersection. Saul is at the right place at just the right time. On the *previous* day, while Saul and the servant were still out in the middle of nowhere looking for those donkeys, God had spoken to Samuel and told him to be on the lookout for this same young man. He gave Samuel an important task— to anoint Saul the king of Israel.

When the two meet, Samuel invites Saul to eat with him, promising to tell Saul *the following morning* what he and his servant wanted to know. And then he adds something strange. "By the way . . . about those missing donkeys. Someone found them and returned them to your father, so you don't need to worry anymore."

Wait. I looked up from the open pages and squinted my eyes at a distant point in puzzlement. *I thought the one thing Saul wanted to know was the whereabouts of* the donkeys. *But the prophet just told him they'd been found. So . . . that* should *be all there is to it. It seems to me like Saul just learned the thing he wanted to know—that the donkeys had been found.*

Apparently God had something else in mind.

Suddenly, it dawned on me. Saul only *thought* this journey was about donkeys. But it was really about so much more.

In these short paragraphs, I saw that God used the problem of rounding up a band of renegade donkeys to put Saul on a collision course with destiny. God moved Saul from his own little world, by means of a frustrating mission, into a place of encounter. A place where God was going to do something extraordinary. *This journey, Saul learned, was never about the donkeys.*

I sat on the couch, with my phone in one hand and Bible in the other, hoping someone would call me with Flash's whereabouts. But the minutes ticked by in silence, so I kept reading. I thought maybe I was getting to the best part and tried to focus on the words on the page instead of thinking about Flash. Out there all alone. With no one to comfort him.

I willed my heart to stop its anxious pace. *Breathe, Rachel.*

The story wraps up with a final scene. The next day, Samuel takes Saul aside and tells him the true reason for his roundup task. He anoints his head with oil, tells him he is going to be king, and reveals what will happen on his way home. He says to Saul, "From this moment on, you'll be changed into a different person." After some final instructions, Samuel sends him on his way. As Saul turns and starts to leave, something amazing happens: *God gives him a new heart.*

Saul's life was forever changed in that moment. His heart was new. He was different. In that instant, he went from being "that tall kid" from an obscure family to being the king of an entire nation. From wet-behind-the-ears bumpkin to powerful leader. He moved from doubt to faith, fear to courage, insecurity to confidence. It was a history-making intersection of obedience and destiny that all started with . . . a donkey problem.

Saul's willingness to take on the unglamorous job of finding some wayward animals put him in the perfect spot for Samuel to find him. It took Saul out of his comfort zone and put him into a place of heart change. God was working behind the scenes the whole time, orchestrating and creating "chance opportunities" that led Saul straight into his purpose and calling.

He was transformed.

Lost donkeys. God's purposes. A date with destiny. I wondered if God might still be in the business of using such humble means for a greater purpose.

If only I *had* a donkey.

Because mine was still missing.

I had fretted when Flash arrived in our lives as a lost donkey, and now it appeared that he'd leave in the same manner. I didn't like the awful irony of it. Not after all we'd been through together.

I thought of his ears—those beautiful ears. And the way his nostrils flared when he was excited about getting a snack. His crazy bray, heard less often these days, but endearing in its earnestness. I loved how he sometimes bucked for joy when we called him in from the field for dinner, and how he liked to follow me around on my exercise walks around his pasture.

I would miss him so terribly if he never came back. My mind was already playing a highlight reel of all of Flash's golden moments, accompanied by Green Day's "Time of Your Life."

Oh, the stories I recalled.

Like the time Flash showed up in the barn with a haircut. A *haircut!* Somehow, some way, his mane had been trimmed into a choppy mohawk. One day he just walked up to the gate with a different hairdo.

We couldn't imagine how it had happened, or more disconcerting, *who* would sneak into our pasture with scissors to chop off his mane. Or *why*. Why would someone give my donkey *spiked bangs?*

We went over the possible scenarios and suspects. Bridgette and Steve, as far as we knew, were out of town. We eliminated them right off the bat, even though we could see how the importance of good hair, at least for a Southern woman, would be ample motivation.

The only other adjoining property was the baby mama's pasture. Perhaps months of watching the pretty little mare become the size of a barge had caused her owner to nurse a grudge, which culminated in taking some scissors to Flash's mane in an act of rage. Like a subtle but crazed message to say, "I'm watching you." It seemed like a strange way to get a message across, but you never know. I mean, he could just call us. We're in the phone book.

Maybe some scissors-happy kid wandered by, and seeing a hapless victim across the fence, decided, "Why not?" Perhaps cutting Flash's mane into ragged strokes fulfilled some kind of dream for him. It could happen.

Or had Flash himself hired someone to come in and give him a new "metro" look? Was he tired of his hipster hair that said, "I can't remember the last time I had a haircut, but since this look is now mainstream with donkeys, it's not cool anymore"? It seemed a plausible explanation, given his love for plaid and vinyl records.

Could it be aliens? Nah. Surely not.

It was like an episode of *Unsolved Mysteries*.

For weeks, we dragged every guest out to see Flash's ridiculous hairdo. We speculated and laughed at the idea that someone would have nothing better to do than trim Flash's mane and then sort of "forget" to tell us. But there *had* to be some explanation!

A couple of months later, when Bridgette and Steve returned from a long vacation and we were catching up, I managed to casually work in the question, "Say, do you know anything about Flash's haircut?" They did.

Bridgette's son, Heath, had been visiting just before they went out of town together, and he had gone over to pet Flash. Flash had rolled in a burr patch, filling his mane with the thorny stickers. So, Heath helpfully cut the burrs out . . . aaand forgot to tell us.

The Mystery of the Phantom Barber solved.

It was only *slightly* disappointing to learn it wasn't aliens after all.

But this wasn't the only mystery Flash had been involved with. There was also the Miracle of the Blue Hoof. That was the time when—

Rrrrring!

Just then, my cell phone rang. It was the sheriff with some news. "Yes? Go on!" Somebody had found a random donkey wandering around and had put him in their pasture for safekeeping. *Could it be Flash? It must be. Please, let it be Flash.* The property was about a mile away, down our twisty road through the woods, over a single-lane bridge, and past a couple of neighborhoods.

I imagined Flash moseying along, searching for that next blade of delicious grass, not realizing he was getting farther and farther from home. I could picture him looking up and not recognizing his surroundings. He must be so scared and lonely! My dear Flash. I felt a small spark of hope as I laced up my shoes and grabbed the truck keys.

The sheriff met Tom and me at the location and gave us that "you again" nod of recognition. I noticed he had a clipboard and was taking notes. I silently willed Flash, if indeed this was Flash, to behave himself in the presence of the law. I certainly didn't want to see his mug shot hanging on the bulletin board of the local convenience store.

Mr. Sheriff escorted us around the house and back to the pasture to see if this stray donkey was ours. My legs felt like jelly as I held my breath.

Flash!

It was him!

His head was over the gate, looking straight at us with his ears pricked forward, just as if he'd been waiting there the entire time. There were the two telltale scars, like choppy lines across his nose. There was the deep scar across his chest and the one on his left shoulder. The small hooves and long, wispy tail. The chocolate-colored cross on his shoulders. The stripe down the center of his back to his tail. The rubbery lips and eager brown eyes. Relief poured over me as I took in every inch of him.

"Is this your animal?" the officer inquired, bushy eyebrows up and pen poised.

"Yessir," we replied in unison, reaching over the gate and caressing his white muzzle. "Yes, this is Flash. This is our donkey." Flash pressed himself close and cocked his head to the side with eyes closed, clearly happy to see us.

"Well, that's some donkey you've got there." The sheriff smiled, putting the pen in his pocket. "I'll let y'all take it from here." He turned to leave, then paused and looked back. "Most strays around here don't have anyone who cares enough to come looking for them. I'm glad this one has a good home."

"Well, he's part of our family," Tom replied. "I wouldn't have believed we'd love a donkey this much, but he's pretty special." He pulled out the halter and lead rope while I wrapped my arms around Flash's neck and squeezed him tightly. I loved his donkey smell—a mixture of dust, grass, sweat, and gentleness.

With a tip of his hat, the sheriff left us to the task of getting Flash home. Maybe he'd come willingly this time.

Or not.

I have no idea how Saul thought that he and one helper could get a whole band of wandering donkeys home from the countryside, because Tom and I couldn't get *one* stray donkey to move twenty feet. Flash dug in his heels and refused to come along. Maybe he was just putting on a show for the horses on the property, trying to impress them with his power to impede. Maybe he wasn't done with his adventure.

Whatever the case, after an hour of coaxing, offering oats, and waiting for him to decide, we were only a stone's throw into our one-mile walk. The sun was starting to set, and Flash was in no hurry to cooperate, despite the fact he was being rescued once again.

"Your donkey needs obedience school," Tom said, adjusting the lead rope in his hands.

"Duly noted." I rolled my eyes at him over Flash's rump from my position at the rear. If we could ever get him home, I'd look right into that. Obviously, we still needed help with our special, much-loved donkey.

The homeowner saw our predicament and offered the use of his horse trailer. Slowly, we urged Flash into it, successful at last. We drove back home, and as we pulled into our pasture and unloaded him, we felt an acute sense of gratitude. Tom was right. Flash wasn't "just a donkey" to us anymore. He was part of the family. He was ours. And, he was a sign. Okay, maybe not a sign, but a *reminder* of something. A reminder of God's providence and care.

I watched Flash pause and take in the scene of his familiar pasture. He breathed the air and sniffed the wildflowers. He nibbled on the tender shoots of grass that poked up from the moist ground, giving a deep sigh as his lips found the next bite. Despite his reluctance to travel, Flash was glad to be back where he belonged. Safe within our care once again. I lingered near him and raised a silent prayer of thanks.

Then it hit me. How many times had I stood in the middle of this very field and talked to God? How many times had I asked for help? Looked up in the sky and prayed for a sign? How many times had I searched Scripture for a message that would meet my need? And how often had God let my gaze fall back upon this stray donkey and given me a picture of His grace and love and guidance? This lost donkey had brought me to a place of encounter with Him more times than I could count.

As a result, I was different. My heart had been transformed. My life was changed.

I closed my eyes for a moment and thought about Saul and how a problem with donkeys had brought him to his destiny. And I wondered about all the "donkey problems" I faced in life. The times I thought, *If I can just figure out what I'm good at,* or, *If I could just change this relationship,* or, *If I could make a whole gob of money.*

I realized how often I made the mistake of thinking that *fixing* things was what the journey was all about. *If I can only "find these donkeys," solve the issue, and get past this problem, everything will work out. I'll go back to my normal life in my little town in obscurity and live happily ever after.*

Maybe we all do this. We wander all over the figurative countryside trying to solve our donkey problems. Our financial setbacks. Our hurting marriages. Our parenting issues. Our soul-killing jobs. Rocky relationships. Ill health. Insecurities. Fears. Doubts. We begin to think we're on a hopeless mission and there is no end in sight. We feel like we have failed. We think we are insignificant. We think God does not see or notice us. We become frustrated with the task.

But what we don't realize is that, even while we're out there in the middle of Nowhereville like Saul was, God has already been at work. In fact, Nowhereville is just where we are supposed to be.

I started to see that all of our donkey problems, our hard situations, are the very things God uses to get us to a place of encounter. A place where our hearts are made new. Like Saul, we've come to the end of everything we can think of to do, and we've given up. And then we give it one last chance, one more shot, and boom. *That's the moment God shows up.* When we're out of our comfort zones, have used up all of our resources, and are at the end of all hope.

That's exactly the place where He meets us. That's just where He'd met me so many times before. And I suddenly knew that it was *through* my circumstances that God had changed me. I'd gone from a starry-eyed dreamer to a wiser, seasoned woman who wasn't afraid of hard work and overcoming obstacles. I went from fear of failing to confidence in His grace. From one who simply read about God's strength in weakness to one who experienced it firsthand. From someone who despised the struggles to one who embraced the lessons found in them. All the situations I tried to fix were simply His means to get me to where He wanted me to be.

I stepped close to Flash and leaned my weight on his shoulders, my arms crossed and chin resting on my hands. "Hey, Donkey Boy. My Flashy."

He brought his head up and turned to acknowledge me, his ears swinging around at the sound of my whisper. The sinking sun made his eyes look warm and understanding as I stroked his smooth brown coat and traced the dark cross on his back with my finger. His mane ruffled in the breeze, the coarse multicolored hair tickling my arm as I circled his neck one more time. Flash blew softly through his lips in a contented *ppphhhfff.*

This journey is never about lost donkeys. Instead, it's always about heart change. It's about transformation. It's about God showing up and making us new.

Lost donkeys.

God's purposes.

A date with destiny.

Your journey isn't about fixing donkey problems.
It's about transformation.

CHAPTER 13

An Unlikely Answer

We had nearly lost Flash, the donkey who had entered our lives as a stray diversion in our busy, overwhelmed world. *Whew. I'm so glad he's back home!*

Feeling gratitude all the way down to my toes, I made sure the pasture gate was closed and the chain was secured. Flash had been following my every move since we returned and now poked his nose over the top rung of the gate for a parting kiss. I laughed at the way his bottom lip jutted to the side as he rested his chin on the gate and gave me that irresistible donkey gaze. You know, the one that implores you for just a bit more attention—and a possible last handout.

"Silly boy." I leaned forward and pressed my lips to his soft muzzle and patted the sweet spot on his nose. "Go on, now." He swung his head up and paused, turning his ears toward me just in case I'd change my mind about leaving. Then he swished his tail and moseyed toward the woods.

Back inside the house, I made a beeline for my office. I grabbed the stack of "Missing Donkey" flyers I'd made, crumpled them, and threw the wadded papers away. Just for good measure, I knotted the trash bag and drove it to the end of the driveway, even though it was a whole day before the garbage collection. I wanted those signs out of the house so I wouldn't be reminded of how close we had come to losing our four-legged family member.

Stepping out of the Explorer, I tossed the bag to the edge of the road and ceremoniously wiped my hands of it. *Done!* But as I turned to get back into the truck, I had second thoughts. I untied the bag and pulled out a rumpled page, smoothing it on my leg. Perhaps it would be good to keep one as a reminder after all. I held the flyer in my hand as I sat behind the steering wheel, parked in nearly the same spot as that first night when Flash had shown up.

What a journey it had been so far!

Dusk had fallen, and as I looked through the windshield at the muddy driveway, my mind relived that cold, bumpy drive home from a job that wouldn't pay our bills. That night, all I had wanted was a warm shower and an end to the struggles we were facing. My heart was too heavy and I was too tired to pray, but somehow, God had heard me.

There, in our headlights, was a mangy donkey.

He looked at us, and we peered back at him, the dust swirling about his feet like smoke in a stage show. Grass protruded from his lips. He swallowed hard.

The donkey did not look like a miracle. He looked like a lot of trouble.

It would have been the easiest thing in the world to simply ignore him, drive up to the house, get ready for bed, and then pull the covers over our heads. Tom and I were tired and discouraged. We weren't speaking to each other. We just wanted to put the day behind us and had every reason to keep going past him. And had we driven on by, I might never have given much thought about a chance encounter with a lowly beast in the road. "Huh, a donkey. That was weird." He would have been the footnote on a tale of a horrid day.

But Tom's seat belt was already unbuckled, and he opened the door. And with one tired sigh and a decision to get out, the game changed.

We *thought* we were rescuing a donkey that night.

But the reality is, God had sent a lost donkey to help rescue *us*. We were the ones needing help. We were the ones who needed to know we were not alone. That God had not forgotten us. That He had a purpose for us. That we mattered to Him.

We needed to know God was with us, and that we could still rely on Him. We needed to know He could reach down and make something good happen, and that He could still speak to ordinary people like us.

So He put a donkey in the driveway.

And we could have driven right by.

But we would have missed the very thing we needed most.

We could not have imagined the answer to our prayers would come in such an unexpected, inconceivable package. Isn't it God's style to provide something wondrous, something newsworthy, something with a little glamour to astound us? That's what I would have envisioned. A package with fuzzy ears, an enormous head, big teeth, and a loud bray? Hardly. But then, God has a sense of humor. Perhaps He knew that it would take a reluctant, lost donkey to illustrate His message to reluctant, lost people like us.

He gave us Flash. Through Flash's example, we learned how to live abundantly in our circumstances, with gratitude and joy. He reminded us to keep breaking down fences to find our passion, and we learned to run with horses and find satisfaction through serving others with love. He taught us to wear our donkey hearts on our sleeves and open up to the world around us. He reminded us to not be afraid of change . . . to let go of the past and embrace possibilities. His donkey trails pointed out that our plodding was really going somewhere after all. He showed us how to make the most of the days we are given. Such priceless lessons.

Flash, in his own inimitable way, taught us how God interacts with His people. I found He uses the everyday parts of our lives to illuminate spiritual truths and to draw us close to Him. I think maybe I'd forgotten that. God's voice is echoed in the stoplights, the grocery store runs, the walks in the park, and the chatter around the dinner table. He calls to us as we do the laundry and the dishes, balance checkbooks, and read bedtime stories.

Do you hear Him? He is in chance encounters with unlikely characters. His presence is nearer than we can imagine. His hand is never far, and His Spirit hovers over us as we go about our daily lives.

Sometimes, we just need to pay attention.

Listen. Observe. Be still.

Unbuckle our seat belts and get out of the car when we'd rather drive on past.

This is what a stray donkey taught us.

But most important, Flash reminded us of God's infinite, unfathomable love. He reminded us that He takes worthless, unworthy, unwilling people and sets His heart on them. On *us*. On you and me. His love makes us valuable, worthy, and beautiful. He heals our scars, He provides for our needs, and He gives us more than we could ask for.

We are His.

We belong to Him.

He calls us by name, and He brings us safely home.

Lessons from Flash

1 Remember your name.
Know whose you are.

2 Know where to find refuge.
True sanctuary is found in God alone.

3 Run with horses.
The pursuit of excellence conquers fear.

4 Find your passion.
Passion leads to purpose.

5 Be a trailblazer.
Persistence makes pathways for grace to follow.

6 Wear your donkey heart on your sleeve.
A well-lived life is an authentic life.

7 Stand where fruit is falling.
The secret of abundance is in choosing gratitude.

8 Be a service animal.
You are made to serve in love.

9 Embrace change.
Don't let fear of the unknown keep you from moving forward.

10 Make things right with others.
Don't miss your chance to forgive, accept, and love.

11 Your journey isn't about fixing donkey problems.
It's about transformation.

Q&A with
Rachel Anne Ridge

What made you decide to write about Flash?

Flash is such a charming, endearing character, how could I *not* write about him? Seriously, I began to notice that I had these little scribbled notes and observations about him in my journals . . . things that began to develop into threads of understanding. I started to see him as my own personal object lesson! I guess I'm a visual learner, and this is how God makes things connect with me. When I wrote about Flash on my blog and saw how he resonated with my readers, it seemed clear to me that he should be the catalyst for the book.

You mention in the book that part of your growing-up years were spent as a missionary kid in Mexico. What was your childhood like? How did your early experiences shape you to be ready for anything life throws your way—whether it's starting your own business or discovering a donkey in your driveway?

Growing up as a missionary kid really did prepare me for being open to new experiences. I loved the colorful culture I was exposed to—the people and the language (and the donkeys) gave me an appreciation for a simpler lifestyle than we typically experience in the United States. I think I've always longed to recreate that with my own family. Living in a foreign country, my parents modeled a view of looking at interruptions as possibilities and seeing inconveniences as opportunities for God to work, and I am deeply grateful for their example. I believe I could have easily missed Flash's lessons without that mind-set of expectation.

Donkeys are often labeled "stubborn" and "ornery." Yet Flash seems to immediately win the heart of (almost) everyone he meets. Why do you think we respond so strongly to him? Do you think all donkeys have people magnetism?

I do think that donkeys are particularly endearing to people! First of all, there's the cuteness factor. Those ears! Those noses! But also, I think there is a humility and gentleness they exude that draws people in. They are extremely social and loyal, two qualities that make for good relationships of any kind. Flash has a huge personality that people respond to, and his adventures make everyone say, "Awww."

The "stubborn" stereotype is one that we "donkey people" are very sensitive to, and we try to educate others about it. Donkeys aren't actually stubborn; they are cautious by nature and will hesitate (or refuse) to do anything they are unsure of. Rather than bolting from a frightening situation like a horse might, they will stop and think about it. They must trust their owner or handler completely in order to do what is being asked of them. Too often, a handler becomes frustrated and will mistreat a donkey, which only creates distrust and exacerbates the "stubborn" myth.

You share in the book about an art teacher who discouraged you at a young age, and as a result it took you years to own your artistic gifts. How did that experience change you? If you ran into that teacher today and got up enough nerve to say anything, what would it be? Did your experience affect the way you guided your own children to discover their interests?

What a sad moment that was! Looking back now, I can only imagine that the teacher may have been preoccupied or may have simply been caught in a bad moment, which had an unintended negative impact on me as an insecure seventh grader. I don't harbor any ill will toward him now, and saying anything to him would not change the past.

That experience has made me very aware of how powerful our words can be, and I've tried to be a positive encourager for my own kids as they've discovered their interests. I always had art supplies, tools, paper, and bits and pieces of things on hand so they could invent and create whenever they wanted. Today, Lauren is a graphic designer, Meghan is a music teacher, and Grayson is on the path to becoming an aerospace engineer—so they've definitely found their niches!

Since Flash joined your family, you've become an advocate for donkey rescue and care worldwide. What have you learned about the importance and social value of donkeys, specifically in developing countries? How can others get involved to help?

I'm so glad you asked! Having Flash has opened my eyes to the great impact donkeys still have on the world, and also the immense need for rescue and welfare. We live in such a modern society here in the United States that we rarely even see a donkey as a pet, let alone as a working animal. Yet there are more than fifty million donkeys in the world, most of whom do the hard work that sustains families and whole communities. Often, these animals are overworked and suffer poor health, which decreases their life spans and their ability to help the people who need them.

One organization whose mission is to aid the welfare of donkeys, horses, and mules is THE BROOKE in the United Kingdom (thebrooke.org). They help some of the poorest communities in the world by providing programs and treatment for their working equines.

THE DONKEY SANCTUARY in the United Kingdom (www .thedonkeysanctuary.org.uk) is well known for its work with donkeys. They foster and adopt donkeys in need and participate in animal welfare work around the world.

SAMARITAN'S PURSE (samaritanspurse.org) provides donkeys (and other livestock) to rural families who need them, particularly in Latin America, Africa, and Asia. Donkeys can pull plows and wagons, haul products, carry water, and provide transportation. They make a huge difference in people's economic lives by allowing them to earn a living and create a future for themselves. I love that.

PEACEFUL VALLEY DONKEY RESCUE in San Angelo, Texas (donkeyrescue.org), is one example of a donkey rescue organization and has facilities around the United States for rescuing, rehabilitating, and finding new homes for donkeys. I've personally visited their facility and even adopted a new donkey friend for Flash from them! They do incredible work for the "forgotten" donkeys of America.

You can help any of these organizations with monetary

donations, and some are looking for hands-on volunteers or people who want to foster or adopt donkeys. They make excellent pets and companions, so you should think about getting one!

In this book, you share with great candor and vulnerability about overcoming your fear of taking risks on new opportunities. What are you doing now that you never would have dreamed of doing before Flash came into your life?

Well, writing a book about a donkey, for one thing! Flash has taught me that my "sixty-two chromosomes" are enough to allow me to "run with horses"! I think of that phrase often, especially as I'm presented with projects and opportunities that scare me, such as speaking to groups and writing a children's book. Facing fear is hard, but it's worth it.

The story of Flash spans some difficult and tumultuous times for your family. Is there a specific quote, thought, or Scripture verse that sustained you throughout?

No matter what happens, it seems I always come back to Psalm 90:17, which has become my life verse:

> Let the beauty of the Lord our God be upon us,
> And establish the work of our hands for us;
> Yes, establish the work of our hands.
>
> PSALM 90:17, NKJV

I created a huge print of this Scripture for our living room so we could see it every day. It was (and is) my prayer for our days—that we would experience God's beauty and favor, and that He would take the work of our hands and make something good happen. Sometimes just breathing this verse as a prayer was all I could do in the midst of my struggles, and I believe God has really been faithful to answer it.

At its core, what would you say the story of Flash is about?

I believe the story of Flash, my raggedy stray donkey, and of our family who took him in, is a story about God showing up in everyone's lives in unexpected ways. It's about being aware that wisdom truly "shouts in the streets" as Proverbs 1:20 describes, and that what we need to do is learn to listen.

I think most of us simply miss the fact that He is reaching out to us, because we're looking for great beams of light and angelic choirs to announce something grandiose. We forget to look at the everyday interruptions, the ordinary occurrences, and the tasks that fill our lives as opportunities to experience God's love and care. I hope that all who read the book will look at their lives in a fresh way and see that the "donkeys" that show up are actually extraordinary gifts in disguise.

What's new with Flash and your family since you completed the book?

I'm so excited to say that Flash has a new buddy—Henderson (aka Henry). He is an adorable minidonkey that we adopted last year. His name comes from the original log-in at the rescue facility, where he was identified as "Henderson #10," the tenth donkey in a roundup in Henderson County, Texas. We simply had to keep the name! He and Flash do everything together, vying for attention (and treats) and generally just enjoying each other's company. It's so fun to see them together!

Life has changed a lot in the past couple of years! Our daughters, Lauren and Meghan, have started their families, and we love being "Nana and Papa" to four little ones. Grayson is finishing up his studies at Texas A&M and is planning for life beyond college. And I've had the privilege of writing two more books! One is a children's book, which is something I've always dreamed of doing—writing and illustrating a story for kids to enjoy with their parents. It stars an adorable donkey named Flash, and it's complete with barnyard friends and adventures. I had a blast creating it! The other is called *Made to Belong: A 6-Week Journey to Discover Your Life's Purpose*. It's a practical and fun study guide/workbook that I hope will inspire readers to step out into their own dreams.

P.S.—Flash started obedience school (otherwise known as donkey-owner training). He is learning to walk on a lead, follow commands, and be loaded into a trailer. He is a (mostly) willing and happy student. I'll keep you posted on his progress. This may take a while.

Follow Flash on flashthedonkey.com, Facebook.com/FlashThe Donkey, and Twitter @FlashTheDonkey.

Acknowledgments

In bringing this book to life, I'm deeply indebted to many people who have made it possible . . .

Priscilla Shirer, my dear, precious friend. Thank you for hiring me to paint Jackson's nursery so long ago. It was a phone call that changed my life. You continually bless me with your encouragement, your insights, and your spur-of-the-moment movie invitations. You are the world's best cheerleader. And Bible teacher.

Bridgette Hawks, my friend and Southern belle. Thank you for letting me share the tender parts of our story, and for being a late bloomer with me. I'm grateful you put that ad in the paper for the charming farmhouse. When we answered it, we got way more than a house—we got an amazing friendship with you and Steve. What a gift.

Ruth Samsel, my incredible agent. Your energy and excitement for *Flash* made this whole project fun. I knew from your first text that we would make a great team. You seem to know just when to push me, and just when to send a little care package to keep my spirits up. It's an honor to be part of William K. Jensen Literary Agency.

Sarah Atkinson, my acquisitions editor at Tyndale Momentum, who fell hard for Flash from the first moment she heard of him. Your commitment to seeing this story become a real book made *me* believe in it. Thank you to the talented team at Tyndale House

Publishers for all of your hard work: Jan Long Harris, Sharon Leavitt, Jillian VandeWege, Nancy Clausen, Cassidy Gage, Maggie Rowe, and Stephen Vosloo. It really tickled me to think about you sitting around together at the office, talking about my donkey. Oh, how I wish Flash could have known he was being discussed in conference rooms—by important people! Then again, he'd never let me forget it.

Bonne Steffen, my editor who made my manuscript sparkle. Sorry for all the sentences that started with *And* and *But*. But somehow you helped me make changes that kept my voice, only better. And you let me keep a few of my "choice" words. You are a master.

Melody Johnson, aka The Donkey Whisperer. Thank you for your expertise and help with Flash along the way.

I'm grateful for my parents, Tom and Anne Rasmussen, who taught me to see past the "interruptions" in life to find what God might be doing behind the scenes. Your faith and example still inspire me every single day. Thank you for your prayers and love.

Lauren and Robert Penn, Meghan and Nathan Miller, and Grayson Ridge: You guys always make me feel on top of the world with your excitement for this book, and for my dreams. I'm very blessed, and more than a little lucky, to be your mom.

Tommy: Thank you for stopping to help a stray donkey one night. It's just so typical of you, and one more reason I love you more than words can say.

Lastly, Flash. Thanks for showing up when you did. You were just what we needed.

Discussion Questions

 Scan the QR code with your phone or visit the link below for a special message to book groups from Rachel and Flash!

http://tyndale.es
/flashintro

1. Have you had a "donkey in the driveway" moment—a time when something unexpected disrupted your life and routine? What was it, and how did you respond?

2. The county sheriff dismisses Flash as "worthless." Do you agree that a living creature can be worthless? Why or why not? Consider some examples from history, the Bible, or your own experiences in which a person (or creature) unvalued by society came to make an impact on the world. What characteristics (if any) do they share?

3. Flash's "ears were a key part of his communication—a silent form of expression that delighted us." What could the Ridges tell about Flash's mood by watching his ears? Think of a friend or family member to whom you're close. What nonverbal cues might you notice that show what that person is feeling—things a casual acquaintance might miss?

4. In chapter 2, Rachel contrasts the names she calls herself (e.g., inadequate, afraid, failure) with the names God gives her (e.g., precious, found, enough). What would your own names be? Write the God-given names on a card and place it where you can see it every day.

5. Think of a time when you, like Flash shivering outside his barn or Rachel suffering a tragic loss, have needed shelter. What were the circumstances? Where was your refuge—the place or people who brought you in out of the cold? What did you learn about yourself, God, and your relationships from that difficult time?

6. What changed for Flash after he had the opportunity to run with horses? What longings or new adventures do you want to pursue in your own life? Does something need to change in your circumstances to make these dreams a reality—and can you begin running after them in some way today?

7. One of Rachel's childhood teachers discouraged her in a way that made a big impact on her life and future. Think back to your own childhood: Did you have a teacher or role model who either affirmed or dismissed your dreams? If the former, how did that encouragement shape your life? If the latter, what changed when you were told you couldn't do it? In what ways does Rachel's own story show that it's never too late to try again?

8. What characteristics do Rachel and Tom show in their endeavors—whether it's learning the ropes at a new business, facing life's challenges, or adopting a stray donkey?

Where in the process do they most struggle, and where do you see them thrive?

9. Consider the many different friendships Rachel describes in the book. Which one resonates with you most and why? If you were to write your life story, which of your own friendships would be most significant to include? How have you learned from each other and grown together?

10. Think of your own pet, either one you have now or a beloved one from your past. If he or she had a "To-Do" list like Flash's, what would be included on it? How has this animal, quirks and all, enriched your life—either through joy or sorrow?

11. "It's safe to say that Flash welcomes change," Rachel says, "just as long as nothing is different or altered in any way." How does his attitude toward change contrast with that of others in the book—Rachel and Tom, Bridgette, even Beau? Who are you personally most like and why?

12. What are some unique things that animals can teach us about love?

About the Author

While tole painting Christmas gifts one year, **RACHEL ANNE RIDGE** discovered a love for art and inadvertently launched a new career. In 1999, she took her paintbrushes and began creating murals and faux finishes in the booming Dallas–Fort Worth area. When the small business started growing, her husband, Tom, joined her. Together, they have expanded into large-scale corporate art, graphic design, wayfinding, and custom artwork. Along the way, they have raised three children; journeyed through loss, failures, and successes; and adopted a stray donkey who showed up on their doorstep and never left.

Rachel began blogging as a means of sharing daily encouragement with other women. Writing about her efforts to create a "soft place to land" for her busy family made a natural connection with an online community of readers who love her gentle wisdom and humor. Since 2006, HomeSanctuary.com has been her blog home, and you can also keep up with her at RachelAnneRidge.com.

Rachel wrote for and managed Priscilla Shirer's blog, GoingBeyond.com, for two years and contributes to other blogs on the topics of parenting, organization, faith, and creativity. She is an engaging speaker who loves to share funny, often poignant stories that touch the heart and reveal God's love in unexpected ways.

Rachel lives in Texas with her husband, Tom, and now, two donkeys.

About Her Donkey

FLASH THE DONKEY enjoys moseying, eating carrots, having his ears scratched, and braying at loud volume when others least expect it. He specializes in Barn Management.

Visit Rachel and Flash online at www.flashthedonkey.com.